Always With You

Always With You

Messages from beyond

Debbie Malone

ROCKPOOL
PUBLISHING

A Rockpool book
PO Box 252
Summer Hill
NSW 2130
Australia

www.rockpoolpublishing.com.au

www.facebook.com/RockpoolPublishing

ISBN 978-1-925017-96-0

First published in 2018

This edition published in 2018

A catalogue record for this book is available from the National Library of Australia.

Cover design by Seymour Design
Internal design by Jessica Le, Rockpool Publishing
Edited by Katie Evans

Typesetting by Envisage Information Technology, India
Cover image by Shutterstock
Printed and bound in China

10 9 8 7 6 5 4 3 2 1

Contents

Always With You

I am only a thought away,
A short distance from you in time,
Although you cannot see me,
I will always give you a sign,

A feather floating from above,
Is a sign from me showering you with love.
The butterfly that flitters near,
Is a sign to show you that I am still here.
The coin you find is not a mistake,
It is from me to you, to pick up as a keepsake.

That gentle breeze you feel beside you,
The touch you feel on the side of your face,
Is a lingering glimpse that I haven't disappeared without a trace.
The familiar thoughts of me that pop into your mind,
Are memories of me that are left behind.

I will always be with you, whether you are near or far.
My light will keep guiding you. I am now your shining star.
Although on my passing there will be a time of separation,
Be assured in the future there will be a time of reunion
And not of desperation.

My love for you will never die,
We will always be in each other's hearts,
Together, you and I.

Debbie Malone

Introduction

It is now nine years since my first book *Never Alone* was released. In that time I have met many amazing people, while doing readings, and I have also lost some amazing people in my life who are now part of the spirit world.

Always With You is a book offering proof of connections from the other side. In writing this book I feel I can confirm to many people that when we die, or pass over, there really is life on the other side. Through my numerous health issues and near-death experiences I have witnessed first-hand that there really is life after this life. To be honest, I find that this is the most exciting thing about life – the possibility of something more.

Always With You offers messages of love, loss and reconnection from the other side. It is about the lengths that our loved ones in the spirit world go to, to reconnect with us and let us know that they have survived what we call 'death'. We should not fear death – it is a part of life and it is a transition until we all meet again in the afterlife.

I have been to the other side and the experience I had was life changing and something I will never forget. I am not frightened of death, but, rather, the manner in which we may experience death.

I hope that you enjoy reading the experiences that my clients, family members and I have experienced when our loved ones have made contact from the other side. The most important thing to remember is this: Our loved ones are always with us and our love never dies.

Chapter 1

Angel In The Car Park

I have always been a pretty skeptical person, but I must state I have also always been very open-minded to the possibility that we are protected from above. I have discovered that if you don't believe anything is possible, you will never discover what truly *is*.

* * *

A few years ago I was a member of a local gym situated near a large shopping centre. The car park of the gym was out in the open and very close to a McDonald's, in a very nice suburb. The gym was very large and was always very busy. Due to family commitments I would visit the gym either in the early hours of the morning or during the evening when my husband would be home to look after our children.

I would often experience an overwhelming feeling of dread and of feeling unsettled whenever I entered or exited the car park. At first I thought that this feeling was just my imagination and I hoped that it would pass.

One morning at 5.30 a.m. as I pulled up into the gym car park I heard a voice whisper in my ear: 'You could get mugged here!' The voice was male and I recognised him as one of my guardian angels. I thought to myself, what an odd message to receive, and pushed the thought aside and continued into the gym to do my workout. When I left the gym the sun had risen and the feeling that something could happen had all but disappeared.

From that day on I began to feel uneasy about going to the gym. I tried to rationalise this fear. To be honest, I didn't really have any reason to feel unsettled at all. However, my gut feeling was to be cautious and be alert coming to and from the car while attending the gym.

Every day afterwards I would hear the same male voice in my ear reminding me of his first warning: 'You could get mugged here!' Each day this message became a little louder than the time before. I began to question whether or not I was imagining things or if there was truly a need for concern.

As time went on my gut feeling became stronger and stronger and my guardian angel kept repeating his words of warning. It got to the point where I would park the car and run up to the gym entrance. It was only once I was on the premises that I felt safe. It was not a good way to be. I was going to the gym to de-stress and yet I was becoming more anxious and stressed about my safety every day.

I am sure while you are reading this you are thinking to yourself, why didn't I just leave the gym or listen to my guardian angel? Even though I work as a full-time psychic medium, it doesn't always mean that I have my

guides and guardian angels on tap. I am also a pretty stubborn person who
literally needs to get hit in the head with common sense before taking action.

After being a member of the gym for another few months the feeling
was just not going away. I wasn't going to the gym as much as I first
had, and my guardian angel's voice was getting so loud it was like he was
screaming in my head: 'YOU COULD GET MUGGED HERE!' It got
to the point where I made an appointment with the gym to cancel my
membership. I couldn't wait for the day to arrive so that I could finally
find some peace of mind.

My appointment time was 7 p.m. on a Wednesday evening in August.
It was a cold and rainy night and the car park was deserted. I entered the
gym and filled out the necessary paperwork to cancel my membership.
I also had to take the tag off my key ring and return it to the office to
complete my cancellation. I hoped that once I had visited the gym for
the last time the feeling of dread that I had been experiencing for so long
would disappear. The only problem was that it didn't disappear, in fact
the feeling became stronger.

That night I went into the shopping centre and purchased some
groceries. I returned to my car with groceries in hand. My car was
parked in a well-lit area near the entrance of the shopping centre, and
the McDonald's restaurant was about 50 metres behind where my car
was parked. I didn't have any need to feel any alarm but something still
just didn't feel right.

I put all of my shopping bags onto the ground whilst I looked
for my car keys in my handbag. As I was fumbling around,
the familiar voice of my guardian angel repeated the words
I had begun to dread: 'You could get mugged here!' This time he was
screaming at me so loudly that I began to feel ill. All of the hairs on the
back of my neck went up and I knew that I was in trouble.

Initially I didn't see what the danger was – I just knew that something was going to happen. By now I was frantically fumbling for my keys when I realised they were in my pocket. I had put them in there after handing in my tag for the gym.

Suddenly, I heard a female voice behind me. She said: 'Can you give me a lift to Hurstville? I will give you twenty bucks?'

I reasoned that it was a female voice, so I should be okay. The thought crossed my mind that females don't mug females, or did they?

At this point I became really angry and thought to myself, this can't be really happening. I had cancelled my gym membership and this was going to be the last time I would be in the carpark in the dark. So why was this happening?

I stood there, frozen, whilst looking straight at this woman. At the same time my guardian angel was showing me images of what her intentions were. My first instinct was to jump straight into the car. The only problem was the central locking would open all doors and my angel showed me that if I jumped into the car then the woman would jump in behind the driver's seat. He then showed me her sitting behind me and grabbing me by the throat.

The woman was dressed in black tracksuit pants and a black sloppy joe. She was about thirty years of age and she had short dyed-blonde curly hair with black regrowth. She was carrying a big black heavy-looking duffle bag over her shoulder. Her eyes were dark and lifeless. The evil energy that surrounded her sent chills up my spine.

At this point a thousand things were going through my mind. I thought, do I run away? Do I scream? Is this really happening? What do I do next?

Suddenly an overwhelming calmness came over me and my guardian angel told me to just stand there and confront her and he would look after me. The woman wasn't too impressed by my apparent calmness. Everything now seemed to be happening in slow motion. She looked at my groceries on the ground. Next she looked at my handbag and then looked at the keys in my hand. She suddenly lunged at me as she attempted to grab my handbag. I looked straight into her eyes and yelled at her: 'Nooooooo!' The voice that came out of my mouth was not my own; it was my guardian angel's voice and it was very deep and masculine. I couldn't believe what was happening, but I knew that my guardian angel was going to look after me in some way, shape or form. He certainly didn't let me down.

The most astonishing thing then took place. Just as the woman was about to grab my handbag a big streak of light came between us. The light was so bright, it looked like a huge bolt of lightning from above. The energy of the light was so powerful that it knocked the woman off her feet. I just stood there dumbfounded. I know that, psychically, I am able to see things, but I was surprised to notice that this woman was also able to see that light. She blinked her eyes and then picked herself up and suddenly jumped back, away from me. She shook her head in disbelief. She then turned away from me and mumbled : 'Where do you live anyway?' Then she mysteriously walked away and disappeared into the darkness.

I couldn't believe that during this whole event there was not another soul in the car park. When the realisation hit me I began to shake uncontrollably. I quickly picked up my groceries, jumped into my car and locked all the doors. I then drove around the car park to see where the woman had gone because I was concerned that she might try to attack another unsuspecting victim. She was nowhere to be found. The whole incident seemed so surreal. But I knew that it had happened.

I once again heard the male voice whispering in my ear telling me: 'You are okay!' He showed me how he had stepped in front of the woman to stop her from causing me harm. I immediately thanked my guardian angel for his love and protection and thought how wonderful it is to know that I am always protected. I will never again doubt that I have an angel by my side.

CHAPTER 2

A Broken Heart

I met Peter Busseler, who had come to me for a reading, on 20 May 2008. During all readings I ask the client to bring a personal item. If they wish to make contact with a deceased loved one, I ask them to bring a photograph of the deceased or an item that belonged to them.

When Peter arrived for his reading he gave me his gold ruby signet ring and a little bulldog soft toy. The bulldog was quite old and looked well-loved – it had a little tear at one of the seams and I could feel how much it meant to Peter. I soon realised that the bulldog had belonged to Peter's father.

The moment I tuned in to the bulldog I could see Peter's father standing beside him. I asked Peter if his father was in spirit and he said: 'Yes, he is.' I explained to Peter how I could see his father standing beside him, on his left side. Peter's eyes lit up when he realised that his father was in the room with us.

Peter then advised me that initially on making his appointment my assistant had given him a different date and time to come and see me. However, there had been an earlier cancellation and my assistant had texted him to see if he would like to move his appointment forward to the 20th of May.

It was only when Peter told his wife of the change of appointment that she reminded him that it was the date of the 1st anniversary of Peter's father's passing. Some people may think that this is a coincidence, but I think that Peter's father had been doing some organising from the spirit world to ensure that Peter was able to see me on such a special day.

L to R: Kurt Bussler with his son Peter before he passed of a heart attack

Peter's father then showed me, from the spirit world, that he had passed from a massive heart attack. He did this by transferring that pain to me so that I understood what he had experienced. The pain was so intense I felt that I was going to pass out. I asked Peter if his father had passed due to heart problems and I relayed the sudden pain that I was experiencing from his father.

Peter sadly replied: 'Yes, he died suddenly of a massive heart attack and I didn't get to say goodbye to him.' Peter's father then began to tell me that Peter needed to be careful as he too had a heart condition that he was not aware of. He wanted me to tell Peter to look after himself better. Peter's father was extremely worried that history was going to repeat itself if Peter wasn't made aware of his situation. He then persisted in telling me to tell Peter that he needed to go the doctor for a checkup.

I asked Peter if he had any been experiencing any heart issues. I had begun to suffer excruciating pain within my own body once again. Since experiencing six Near-Death Experiences I have been given the ability to connect with my clients' bodies when they have health issues. I can either see the issue inside the client's body (it glows), or I can feel it within my own body. I always advise the client that I do not have any medical training whatsoever and the messages I am picking up are from spirit. I am always careful about how I pass this information on because it can sometimes be quite scary and confronting to the client. If I see or feel something, I ask the client if they are experiencing any discomfort and I relay to them the area where I feel or see the pain in their body. If they agree that they are experiencing issues then I gently suggest to the client that it might be a good idea to visit their local doctor to seek medical advice, just in case there is an issue that they are not aware of.

In Peter's case I didn't have much choice because his father was being very persistent in encouraging me to give his son the information. Peter said that he didn't have any health issues that he was aware of and he told me that he exercised regularly and felt as fit as a bull. Yet again, his father persisted in telling me that Peter should go to the doctor to have a checkup. Once again I passed on the information and then I tried to continue to give Peter a reading. By this time I felt that Peter was getting a little annoyed with me.

I could see that Peter had recently sold his business and he was about to retire. I could see the future life that Peter wished to have with his wife and children. Peter's father showed me images of his grandson and he showed me Peter guiding his son in his own business venture. Peter's father was so proud of Peter and showed me what a great father he was to his two boys. I felt that Peter was about to begin a new chapter in his life and as I passed on the images of his future to him his dad abruptly stepped in again and asked me AGAIN to tell his son that he had a health issue.

This time I could suddenly see inside Peter's body and I could see three blockages in Peter's heart. The blockages were at the back of the heart muscle. I explained to Peter that I could see and/or feel health issues within clients' bodies as if it were happening to my own body. (It doesn't happen to everyone I do a reading for; it only happens if it is vitally important for me to pass on the knowledge to the client.) I also explained to him that in no way, shape, or form did I think I was a doctor with medical knowledge. I just wanted him to know what I was seeing and that he should at least pay attention to what I was being shown. It would then be up to Peter to have a checkup.

Still Peter's father would not stop nagging me about how important it was for Peter to listen to me. His father then asked me to remind Peter that he had died of a massive heart attack and he did not want Peter to suffer the same fate.

I was then shown an image of Peter's family, as in a photograph, and there was a blank space where Peter's father should have been standing. The image then changed to a photograph of Peter standing with his wife and children and the image of Peter began to fade. This image greatly concerned me, so I wanted to ensure that I did all I could to change the outcome.

I wish to point out that we are all assigned a time here on Earth. I see life as if it is like sand running through an hourglass. Unfortunately, some of us are given more sand in our hourglass than others. My journey in life is to ensure that each person I meet who seeks my advice or guidance is given the choice to choose whether or not they wish to use every grain of sand in their hourglass.

After I passed on the message about Peter's heart issue yet again, I apologised for the persistence and told him that I would try to leave that topic, and tune in to other areas of his life.

The next image I could see was a big fishing boat – the type you would use if you were going deep-sea fishing. When I saw this image I felt that Peter was about to go away with some mates, on a fishing trip. The image was very clear and I could feel that this was an event that Peter was very much looking forward to.

I asked Peter if this information made sense to him and he relayed that he would be going deep-sea fishing with some friends in two weeks' time, to Swains Reef in Gladstone. I then heard his father say very loudly in my ear that Peter would not be going on the trip, as he would be in hospital having heart surgery.

I didn't really know how to relay this news to Peter because I knew how much he was looking forward to the trip and I could see that the weekend was booked and paid for. I yet again said I was worried about his heart. I found it hard to tell him that I could see him in an operating theatre undergoing heart surgery.

I once again told him that he REALLY, REALLY, REALLY needed to go to the doctor and have a checkup. (By this time I am sure Peter thought I was becoming a bit of a nag.) Peter just smiled and said: 'Yes, I heard you. I will go and get a checkup.'

We spoke further about Peter's father and how he was very well aware of how Peter's life has been since his father's passing. His dad wanted Peter to know how proud he was of him and he wanted to thank Peter for all he had done for his mother. His father wanted Peter to clean up all of his unfinished paperwork.

Peter's father also wanted Peter to know how much he missed being with the family, especially being a part of his grandsons' lives. He showed me how proud he was of Peter, as a father himself, and the connection that Peter and his two sons shared, like Peter shared with his own father.

The reading came to a close and his father reiterated that Peter really should go and see a doctor. Peter agreed that due to my constant nagging he would take my advice and visit his local doctor.

* * *

A few months after doing the reading for Peter, I had some feedback about what had transpired. The way the information came back to me was quite strange in itself because it was not via Peter, but via my husband. My husband, Warwick, is a builder and had been working on a job site when another tradesman – a plumber – came over to him and said: 'I want to talk to you about your wife.' He then asked: 'Is your wife's name Debbie Malone, and is she a psychic/medium?' My husband said, 'Yes, she is.' The man then proceeded to say that I had done a reading for his friend Peter who was a retired electrician. He then told my husband that I had saved Peter's life.

He relayed how Peter had come to see me for a reading to make contact with his father in spirit. Peter had told his mate that he hadn't expected for me to pass any messages on to him about his health because he was fit and healthy, or so he thought. The plumber also told my husband that Peter had been booked to go on a deep-sea fishing trawler for a week of fishing with his mates. He told my husband that when I did the reading for Peter I had informed him numerous times that he needed to get his heart checked because I could see that there was something wrong.

He said Peter did listen to my advice and made an appointment with his doctor. After having a CT scan and then an angiogram of his heart, three blockages were discovered. Consequently, Peter did not go on his deep-sea fishing trip; instead he was quickly admitted to hospital to have heart surgery.

When my husband arrived home later that day, he said to me: 'I saw a guy at work today and he said, "I want to talk to you about your wife!"' I thought to myself, Uh, Oh what have I done! He then told me that I had saved Peter's life! He then relayed the conversation he had with the plumber earlier that day.

I would like to point out that when I do readings I don't always remember all of the details of the information that I pass on to the client because I channel the information then release it when I have passed it on to the client. However, in Peter's case, the heart issues and the deep-sea fishing were quite a distinct memory that was still very clear in my mind.

I was so happy to hear that Peter did listen to my advice and that he sought the appropriate medical intervention to check his heart. I do understand that the essence of life can change at any given time. I am so grateful that Peter was given time to utilise the sand of his hourglass.

Sometimes I question why I am given information to assist a client when I can't directly change their outcome if they don't heed the advice. I have come to accept that we all have free will and I am only the messenger; the rest is up to the client.

What struck me the most about this situation with Peter was that we had six degrees of separation. It was so random that my husband was working with a mate of Peter's and it was through him that I found out about Peter's operation. I wondered if Peter would ever return to see me after the heart surgery, to personally tell me his story.

Approximately twelve months after Peter had heart surgery he did return to see me for a reading. When Peter walked into the room, I could see his father in spirit standing by his side, with a huge smile on his face. His father whispered in my ear: 'Thank you.'

Peter told me that after the reading he had discussed it with an old Irish workmate. The workmate then told Peter that his family who still lived in Ireland was also 'gifted', that they had psychic abilities and could see spirits. He then admitted to Peter that he had had a dream of Peter lying on the floor holding his heart. He told Peter that he was concerned about him but had been worried about telling him because he was unsure of how Peter would react.

Peter went to his local doctor to ask if he could see a heart specialist. When the doctor asked Peter why he wanted to see a heart specialist, Peter did not want to admit to the doctor that a medium had spoken to his dead father, who told him that he had a heart issue. Thankfully, the doctor agreed to Peter's request due to the family's history of heart attacks. Also, Peter had high blood pressure and was under a lot of stress due to his previous business.

When Peter went to visit the cardiologist he underwent a stress test and an ultrasound of his heart. He was told by the cardiologist that there weren't any apparent problems and that there was nothing wrong with him.

Peter then asked if there was any additional testing he could undertake and asked if he could have a second opinion. The cardiologist then asked him why Peter was so concerned. Peter then explained to the cardiologist that a medium had told him he had a problem with his heart. The cardiologist shook his head in disbelief at Peter and advised that Peter could have an angiogram. He explained to Peter that the test was invasive and that a tube would need to be inserted into his groin up to his heart. The other option was a heart CT scan, which would be more expensive but less invasive.

Peter underwent the CT scan and within a few days he received a call from the cardiologist's office asking him to come in. After receiving the results from the heart CT scan the cardiologist insisted that Peter have an angiogram. The test results had shown an overall 70 per cent blockage and two further 50 per cent blockages in his heart. This is all after the cardiologist had initially deemed nothing wrong!

The cardiologist told Peter that he was very surprised by the results – Peter had also recorded a high range of 'calcium markers', which indicate coronary artery disease, causing plaque deposits on Peter's artery walls.

Peter had the angiogram on the following Tuesday. There was just one problem, though: Peter and his mates had booked to go on their deep-sea fishing trip twelve months prior and Peter was about to leave on the Saturday, which was only three days after his angiogram. Peter was insistent that he was still going on his trip despite the cardiologist's warning that this could be a dangerous decision, considering that he would be isolated on a boat in the middle of the ocean.

Peter didn't go on his fishing trip, after all. I personally think it was due to Peter's father's intervention. A cyclone developed on the coast of Queensland, off Gladstone, where the trip was due to depart. Due to the intensity of the cyclone the coast guard prohibited all commercial vessels from leaving the harbour until the cyclone had passed, so the fishing trip was cancelled and all of the men's deposits were returned.

Peter was asked by the cardiologist to contact him on Friday to receive the results of his test. The cardiologist informed Peter that he needed to have heart surgery because there was a 95 per cent blockage in one artery and two 30 per cent blockages in two other arteries.

Peter now has yearly heart checkups with his cardiologist and, to this day, everything looks fine.

* * *

After Peter relayed this information to me you could not wipe the smile off my face. I was so happy that Peter's time here on Earth had been prolonged due to his beautiful father's warnings. Peter's heart is in fine shape because of his father.

Peter said to me that I had helped to save not only his life, but also his friend's. I asked Peter how this could be. Peter then explained that he had spoken to a friend of his and told him about the events that he had experienced with his heart and how he had heart surgery to insert a stent and clear the blockages in his heart.

This friend then told another friend of theirs about what Peter had just experienced. Funnily enough, this friend had been feeling unwell for a while, so he decided that he should also go and see his doctor. Thankfully he did. He was diagnosed with a condition known as the 'widow maker'. This condition can prove to be fatal. He also underwent heart surgery and found out that he had a 99 per cent blockage in his heart, which resulted with him also having a stent inserted.

The term 'widow maker' refers to a specific type of <u>heart attack</u> that is known to have grave consequences. It is called this because those who suffer one often die, and the wives of affected men, therefore, often become widows.

* * *

It never ceases to amaze me how our loved ones in spirit are always with us, guiding and protecting us, even though at times we may doubt that they are there. When we pass over our love never dies and we never forget those here on Earth.

I feel so blessed that I have been given the opportunity to speak with loved ones in spirit and to be able to help and guide those of us in the living world. Peter's father is certainly the hero of this story – if it were not for him, Peter may have joined his father in spirit much sooner than was necessary.

I am so happy to see that Peter has more time here on Earth with his beautiful wife and two loving sons.

CHAPTER 3

Wings From Heaven

In November 2010 I was working at the Mind Body Spirit festival in Sydney, conducting personal readings for clients, via psychometry.

During the four festival days I did two readings that turned out to be very significant to the Sommerville family. The first reading was for Anne Sommerville. Anne sat down in front of me and handed me her jewellery. This was to help me 'tune in' to her life. Her father Neil appeared. Her father's energy was very strong and I could feel how excited he was that I could see and hear him so clearly. I asked Anne if her father was in spirit and she confirmed that he was.

The first thing Neil said to me was that he wanted me to draw a picture for his daughter. So I quickly grabbed a business card and, on the back of it, drew the images he was showing me.

The images were of a girl's face and wings situated inside a heart with angels' wings also on either side of the heart. Neil then showed me another image of what I felt was a brooch or pendant with a heart in the middle and angel wings on either side. I wasn't sure what these images meant, however I knew it was a very important message that he wanted me to relay to his daughter.

This is the drawing of the brooch I drew for Jessica while connecting with her grandfather Neil Sealby

The Angel Wing brooch that Neil made

I asked Anne if she knew anything about the images I had drawn and if she knew about a piece of jewellery that fitted the description. Anne answered that she wasn't aware of anything that looked like the drawing.

I then asked Anne if her father had served during a war, as Neil showed me an image of him standing proudly in his military uniform, with his military medals pinned on the left-hand side of his chest.

Anne acknowledged that her dad had served in New Guinea during the Second World War.

Neil then showed me images of his life during the war. He told me how hard it had been to be away from his family. Neil was a loving family man and he said the thought of coming back home to Australia was what helped him get through his days in New Guinea. He told me his greatest concern during the war was whether or not he would make it back home to be with them again. Thank goodness he lived to return.

During the rest of the reading Neil wanted me to share messages of the love he had for his family and his daughter. He wanted Anne to know how proud he was of his beautiful granddaughter, Jessica, and wanted to let Anne know that he was with the family all of the time and was very much aware of their lives, since his passing.

The most important message he had was that he missed his beautiful wife, Jean, dearly and wanted his daughter to pass this sentiment on to her. He wanted Jean to know that he loved her as much now as he did on the day they were married. He gently reminded me that he wanted his daughter, Anne, to make sure that she took the card with the drawing on it to show her mother. Anne carefully put the card into her wallet so she could relay the messages from her father.

The reading drew to a close and Anne stood up to leave. When she did this her wallet flew out of her hands and the contents of the wallet scattered all over the floor. Together we picked up all of the items and Anne put everything back into her wallet (or so we thought).

It wasn't until after Anne had left that I discovered the drawing of the angel-wing illustration sitting behind the chair on the floor. I picked up the card and sat it on the table where I was conducting the readings.

The next person I did a reading for was a young lady named Jessica, (unbeknownst to me Jessica was Anne's daughter).

As soon as I held Jessica's jewellery Neil appeared again, behind her. I then realised that Jessica was Neil's granddaughter. Neil was very persistent and kept pointing to the card on the table. I promptly told Jessica that her grandfather was with her and he was standing behind her. I told Jessica that her grandfather wanted me to give her the card with the drawing on it. I then explained that I had drawn the pictures for her mum during her reading, but Neil obviously hadn't wanted Anne to have them because he felt they were a special gift to Jessica. (I now understood why Anne's wallet fell from her hands, making the card fall out of the wallet.)

Neil told me to tell Jessica what I had told her mother. Neil then spoke about the piece of jewellery he had made while he was serving in the Second World War and he said that if Jessica found out where the jewellery piece was, he wanted her to have it because he felt that she was his little angel.

I asked Jessica if she had ever seen the item I had drawn and Jessica also replied that she had never seen it.

Neil proudly told me about his beautiful granddaughter Jessica and he wanted her to know how proud he was of her. I could see that Jessica was very artistic and I began to see images of drawings, cartoons and animations.

I kept seeing the characters from the movie *Toy Story*. I was then shown an image of the desk lamp that is the logo for Pixar Animations.

I passed this message on to Jessica and her eyes lit up. Jessica informed me that she had applied for a Student Volunteer program in Los Angeles, in America, called the SIGGRAPH Conference. SIGGRAPH is an international conference for computer animators, game designers and computer wizards. I told Jessica that I could definitely see a connection to the Conference and to Pixar.

The reading came to an end and I could feel Neil gently reminding me to make sure that Jessica speak to her nan, Jean, to ask about the drawing.

I continued working at the Mind Body Spirit festival over the weekend, however this reading really stayed in my mind. Neil stayed with me for a few days and this is what he told me about the drawing:

Neil said that while he was serving in New Guinea he worried that he might not return home to his family. He decided that he wanted to make something very special as a memory of his time overseas.

Neil then showed me the effort he went to, to handcraft the brooch that I had drawn for his daughter Anne and granddaughter Jessica. Neil told me that he had found an abalone shell on a beach in New Guinea while he was serving in the war. He then showed me how, with the limited tools he had available to him, he had carved the shell into the shape of wings. Neil was very proud of how he had made the heart in the centre of the brooch, from a flattened out bullet casing.

I hoped that Jessica would find the piece of jewellery that I had described and drawn. I let the thought go and felt that only time would tell.

* * *

This is the email I received from Jessica after the reading:

Hi Debbie,

After my reading I showed the picture to my nan, asking if she had ever seen a piece of jewellery that looked like it. She said she had and she brought out a box and handed me a brooch. It looked exactly the same as your drawing. Nan started to tell the story behind the brooch. My grandfather, while he was fighting in New Guinea during World War Two, had fashioned the brooch by carving the wings out of a mother-of-pearl shell, and the heart shaped from an empty bullet casing. It must have been very sentimental to my grandfather, since he carved it himself. I explained the story to Nan and she gave me the brooch to keep. This incident has greatly changed my outlook on many things in life.

Kind Regards,
Jessica

* * *

I love having the gift of making contact with loved ones on the other side, connecting them with their loved ones amongst the living. Every reading I do never ceases to amaze me, as the information that those in spirit share with me gives me proof that life never ends and spirit endures all.

I have met Jessica and Anne over the last couple of years at the Mind Body Spirit festivals since that very first reading. The insight that Neil has about his family, especially Jessica, is amazing.

Jessica did get to meet people from Pixar when she went to the SIGGRAPH Conference in Los Angeles. She is now working as a computer animator in a company in Sydney.

* * *

Before the publication of this book, another part to this story unfolded. Unfortunately, Jessica's beautiful nan, Jean, passed away on 5 March 2015 of bladder cancer. Jean had only been diagnosed with the cancer a short time prior to her death. Jean's passing was a great tragedy for the Sommervilles because she was such an integral part of their beautiful family.

After Jean's death, Jessica said that she was reading letters from her grandfather, Neil, to his mother back in Australia. During his time in New Guinea he was a bachelor, so it was a bit of a mystery as to whom Neil had made the brooch for.

What was his intention when he created the brooch? Was it to give to his future wife when he met her? No doubt this was probably on his mind while he was fighting overseas:

This is one quote from one of the letters he wrote to his mum:

The fourth day, which is today, Sunday, is in a way a rest day, in other words washing day. Seeing that nothing else has happened I must finish up now, Mum, as that washing won't do itself and I must get them dry. Don't you think I would make an ideal hubby for some lonesome female?

On his return from the war he met and married his beautiful bride, Jean, in 1949 and they lived happily ever after until Neil's passing in the year 2000.

Since Jean has passed over I have received some messages for Jessica. The most important one being that Neil came to meet Jean. They are so happy to be reunited in spirit and they are, and always will be, an integral part of Anne and Jessica's lives. Jean cheekily reminded me to ensure that Jessica takes the time to get outside amongst nature, as this is how she intends to make contact with her beautiful granddaughter. As I write this I see a beautiful image of coloured butterflies dancing around Jessica in the garden. Jean has now been given her wings and she has transitioned from this life into the next; she has the freedom to come and go as she pleases. Most importantly Neil and Jean are together again.

Jean and Neil Sealby (Jessica's maternal grandparents)

One last message from Jean and Neil to their beautiful Jessica is that they both can see that she has an amazing future ahead of her and they are so proud of the beautiful young woman Jessica has become. The greatest gift they can now give Jessica is their guidance, as they are now her Wings From Heaven.

CHAPTER 4

Endless Love

I briefly met John and Carole Boardman at their women's fashion store, 'Emma James', in Gymea, some years before Carole passed away in February 2011.

At the time I didn't realise just how significant this brief meeting would become and how the connection between the Boardman family and me would be in the future.

This chapter is about the Endless Love between John and Carole Boardman and the fact that no matter what happens after death, love will find a way to get through to those who are left behind.

In September 2011 I reconnected with John Boardman when he had booked in for a reading. My office doorbell rang and I opened the door to John, who was at the time a well-dressed man in his sixties. I recognised his face but I couldn't work out where I had seen or met him before.

I asked him to come in and take a seat in the room where I conduct readings for clients. John said that he was a bit skeptical and he was nervous about coming to see me. He apologised and said that another lovely client of mine named Kathy had told him to come. Kathy had lost her beautiful husband and had come to see me to reconnect with him after his passing. She thought that it would be a good idea if John came to see me so I could reconnect him with Carole.

John sat down and I asked him if I could hold a piece of his jewellery. He took off his gold wedding ring and a smaller gold ring for me to hold. As soon as I held the rings I could feel that his wife was in spirit.

I was instantly shown a lot of paperwork that looked like legal papers and I relayed the image to John. He said that Carole hadn't wanted to leave as she had lots of paperwork to attend to.

Carole showed herself to me when she was sick and I could see her hair was very thin. I began to smell the strong aroma of cigarette smoke and I felt that there was something wrong with her chest area. I found it hard to breathe and all I could smell and taste was cigarette smoke. My parents smoked when I was growing up and I absolutely hate the smell of smoke. My grandfather had also died of throat and lung cancer and I was very familiar with the smell of smoking that I was picking up.

John said that his wife, Carole, had died of lung cancer. Carole then began to show me an image of herself when she was younger. She was sitting and holding a cigarette between the fingers on her right hand, in a glamorous pose as though she was a Hollywood movie star. She then told me that when she was younger it was quite glamorous to smoke. Carole said that she didn't ever think that smoking would take her away so early from John and her children.

I heard the message: 'Bad things happen to good people!' I repeated this back to John and he agreed that this was the case. Carole then said to me that she knew people who had smoked all their lives and had died at a ripe old age; however, this was not the case for Carole and for her family.

Carole showed me what she looks like now that she is in spirit. I could see that her thick auburn hair had returned, and she looked extremely well. It was important for me to give this message to John because she knew how worried he had been seeing her deteriorate as the cancer progressed. Carole told me how hard it was for her to see John suffering through her illness. She said that she had always hoped that the doctors had made a mistake and that, by some miracle, she would recover. She told me that during her illness she had hoped that it was all a horrible dream that she would wake from.

The love I felt between this beautiful couple was overwhelming; the sadness of the loss was almost too much to bear. I could see that John and Carole were soulmates and the sadness they both experienced affected me greatly.

Carole and John Boardman

I could see that Carole was a bit feisty at times and she wanted me to tell John that she was sorry for giving him a hard time when she got a bit grumpy towards the end of her life. John agreed with me that Carole was hard on him. She repeated to me how sorry she was and she wanted me to tell him how much she truly loved him.

I was suddenly shown an image of a house. I asked John: 'What is going on with the house?' John replied: 'Nothing is going on with the house . . . I am not selling it.' John said that they had discussed this before Carole passed away.

Carole then showed me an image of her at home, now that she is in spirit. She told me that John sees glimpses of her in the back room when he is watching television. John says that he actually turns around to talk to her and realises that she isn't there. Carole told me that she wants him to talk to her. She hears and sees what is going on with him and the family.

I described the room where I saw Carole. I told John that this room is very special to her and it brought her a lot of joy. The room is at the back of the house and it is bright and sunny. I had visions of John and Carole having a cuppa and I saw them talking and laughing.

John told me that this room is at the back of his house and he said this was Carole's favourite room. Carole specially designed the room before it was built. John said that the room was also the room in which she spent a lot of time before her passing.

The images in my mind suddenly changed and I was shown inside Carole's body where there was scarring on her chest area. I asked John if Carole had any scaring on her body or her lungs?

John replied: 'No, but she had major heart surgery at the age of ten – this left big scars on her body around that area.' I received the impression that Carole had had a challenging childhood and I felt her life really began when she met John.

Carole began to show me images of how sad John was after her loss. She said to me that it is very tough for him without her.

I could see that John wished that he was with her and it was difficult at times for him to even think of a life without her. Carole whispered in my ear that John feels guilty about living because she is not there. I relayed this message to John: 'Carole wants you to live on for the children.' I asked John: 'Do you have a daughter?' John replied: 'Yes, I have a daughter, Emma, and a son, James!' I began to feel overwhelmed by the images that popped into my head.

I felt the excitement building as we spoke about Carole and John's precious children. Carole then showed me a wedding and told me that she was present at Emma's wedding. She said that she would never miss an opportunity to 'frock up'. John laughed. John and Carole owned a fashion boutique before her passing and he told me that Carole always dressed immaculately, and that if she had been alive she would have looked beautiful.

I was given an image of a tropical island and I saw that this is where the wedding took place. I relayed this message to John and he said that Emma was married in Fiji.

Carole said that the wedding had been an extremely difficult time for John because Carole had died in February 2011 and Emma was married in June 2011. Carole had hoped that she would have lived long enough to see her daughter walk down the aisle. I could see that John had reservations about attending the wedding as he was still trying to cope with the loss of Carole.

Carole was extremely happy that John did attend and she wanted him to know that he was not alone. She laughed and said that he couldn't get rid of her that easily. John replied that he hadn't wanted go in the two weeks leading up to the wedding because he didn't want to go without Carole.

Then Carole began to tell me how cranky she is with John. She wanted me to tell him that he should never feel guilty because he is still here and she isn't. I suddenly saw Carole holding a beautiful baby girl in her arms. Carole looked up and smiled at me and said to tell John about their beautiful baby granddaughter who was on her way. She said that she was looking after her until Emma was ready to have her. I was given the image of a calendar with 2013 on it. Carole cheekily told me that Emma had better get a hurry on! I relayed this to John and he replied: 'That would be fantastic!'

Carole then told me that there are baby girls coming and she said that the little one she is nursing is coming by-hook-or-by-crook. She then expressed how angry she was about leaving the family so early. She so wanted to be there for the weddings and the grandchildren. John told me that while Carole was in hospital, before her passing, she was given the wonderful news that their son, James, was getting engaged. As he said this Carole suddenly popped an image of a cruise ship in my head. I asked John if he and Carole had discussed plans of going on a cruise prior to her death. John said that unfortunately, due to Carole's illness, they never went on the cruise they had talked about – because she passed away before they got the chance.

After sharing this information with John, Carole continued to show me the image of a boat, only this time the image was of a motorboat and not a cruise ship. The feeling I got when I saw this image was of happiness and beautiful memories. John then told me that Carole's father had owned boats when Carole was a child. Her father had actually raced motorboats and had owned a few racing- and leisure boats before his passing.

Carole also showed me happy memories of a location, which I felt was on the South Coast of Sydney. John said that Carole had very happy memories of this place – her family had always taken their boat with them when they went down to the NSW South Coast for holidays with her family. At this point of the reading I saw Carole between the ages of 9–13 years. She had long auburn hair and she was riding a horse. I saw an image of her with her hair flying in the wind and she was so happy. I also saw another image of her in her thirties, horse riding with great delight; however John did not share Carole's enthusiasm of horse riding.

Carole began to tell me how stressed John had been about getting things cleared out of the house. Carole wanted me to tell him that he just needs to take his time and to do things when and if he feels ready. I could see that friends and family had been giving him advice and prompting him to sort out Carole's things, which was making him upset. Carole would be with him to help him when the time was right.

Carole showed me how much she loved their garden and she showed me an image of John in the garden with her by his side. John's face lit up when I told him this as he had felt her presence whenever he had done the gardening.

John had a moustache. Carole suddenly showed me an image of John shaving it off. Carole pleaded with me to tell John not to shave off his moustache. John looked at me quite shocked and asked me how I knew about that. He told me that, over the last couple of days, he had decided that 'Yes' he was going to shave it off. He said that he hadn't told ANYONE about his decision and couldn't quite believe that I knew anything about it. I just smiled and said that this was confirmation that Carole was always with him.

I asked John what had he done with the clothesline? I had been given the image of the clothesline being put in another part of the garden. I asked John had he moved it or something? John looked at me blankly and said: 'Gee, I don't understand that one.' I told John that sometimes during a reading things don't always make sense. I said that it might make sense to him when he gets home and thinks about it further. (John rang me a few days after his reading and told me that he had forgotten that the clothesline had been moved from its usual position so that a marquee could be erected for Carole's wake.)

Carole began to tell me that there was an issue with her ashes after her cremation. I asked John: 'What was the dilemma with Carole's ashes? She is telling me that something happened.' John said: 'Yes, there was a problem with the name plaque. It took twice as long to be made as it should have. It was very stressful for me at the time.'

Carole then showed me the image of John driving to Woronora Cemetery to visit her and then him getting back in the car to drive home. What John doesn't know is that Carole gets into the car with him and goes with him to comfort him and then when he leaves she gets back into the car and comes back home with him. When I relayed this to John he began to smile. Carole cheekily told me that the reason she does this is because she is not going to hang around the cemetery with all of those dead people when she can be at home with her soulmate John!

Carole showed me that since her passing John had changed his car. She started to laugh and told me that she was stirring him up about this. John replied: 'Yes, I bought a car the same as my son's car as we are keen on our cars.' John then explained that he and his son James have the exact same car, in the same colour, which he purchased after she passed.

I told John that Carole said she still went for drives with him – she wanted him to know that it was because the two of them were so connected. This information made John feel quite emotional and he told me that it made him want to cry.

Carole then gave me the image of a 'knight in shining armour' and I saw the image of a 'damsel in distress'. I asked John if he related to what I saw. He replied: 'Yes, Carole told me that I rescued her from an ugly situation before we were married.' Carole's parents had both passed away before she was fifteen years of age and she had been left in the care of relatives. Carole showed me images of home movies playing on a television screen. I saw little children running around playing with a younger version of Carole and John. I asked John if he had any videos of their children. He replied: 'Yes, from a very early age we have a video of them. We played the video to Carole on a laptop computer while she was in hospital.' Carole wanted me to let him know how happy she was that the family had done this before her passing.

I then saw images of a suburb called Oatley. I recognised the location and asked John about this. The happiness that I felt at this memory was overwhelming. John told me that when they first got married they had a house there. He said that they were really happy times. He said that they also had their second shop at Oatley. I told John that I couldn't believe how persistent Carole was – how adamant she was in giving me proof of life after death, to share with him.

The entire reading was recorded on an audio tape. When John got home and replayed the tape he was shocked by what he heard. When I was telling him that she was trying to give him survival evidence ('survival evidence' is proof of life after life), the sound of a heartbeat could be heard on the tape. To this day John still can't believe what happened on his tape. I don't think he is skeptical anymore.

* * *

Since my first appointment with John, I have seen him on numerous occasions. It never ceases to amaze me the effort that Carole goes to, to get her messages across.

Over the years I have been known to run ghost tours at Picton in New South Wales. On one of the Picton tours John booked in to come along for the night. My son, Blake, also came along for the tour. I offered to collect John because his home was on my way to Picton, and this would save him the drive to Picton on his own.

Blake had no prior knowledge of John or his family so I found it very interesting how he too felt the very strong presence of Carole during the night. After I had collected John I could smell the strong aroma of smoke in the car. As neither John, Blake or I smoke, I knew only too well that Carole was coming along for the night. When we arrived at Picton, Blake pulled me aside and asked me why the car smelt so badly of smoke. He absolutely hates the smell of smoke, like I do, so I found it amusing that he was picking up on Carole's presence.

During the night of the ghost tour we had a lot of ghostly activity. As this was Blake's first ghost tour with me I wondered what he would pick up. At the end of the evening after we'd dropped John home, Blake began to tell me about the lady who had been with him all night. He described the woman as having auburn hair, brown, almond-shaped eyes and a gentle smile. He told me that he thought she was John's wife and he said that she smoked. He told me that he had experienced a sore chest and had found it hard to breathe. I explained to him that this woman was indeed John's wife and her name was Carole. He then told me that the entire evening he could see Carole by John's side. She had told Blake that she wanted John to know that she was okay and that she loved him very much.

I found it interesting that Carole had now also made contact with Blake in order to give John confirmation that she was still with him. Blake said that he was too embarrassed to tell John what Carole had said because he didn't know John very well.

The following morning I rang John (I hoped the timing was right) and told him what Blake had experienced. I passed on her messages and John was extremely thankful.

* * *

I have also seen Emma and her husband, Chris, and James and his wife, Lyndall, for readings. Each and every time Carole comes through loud and clear to her beautiful growing family.

Carole is aware of the new additions to the families and of the progress the boys have made working in their own business.

Carole was right in sharing the knowledge with me about the baby girls, who were waiting in spirit to join her children. Amelia Zoe Voyce was the first granddaughter to arrive, in February 2013. This was a few days before the second anniversary of her beloved grandmother in spirit. Carole told me that this precious gift was to help ease the family's pain when each anniversary came around.

Amelia is a beautiful little girl who is very aware of her grandmother's presence. Carole tells me that this is the little one I saw her holding so many years ago.

Chloe Isla Voyce arrived in December 2015. Chloe's arrival was to help the family get through Christmas without Carole by their side.

Charlotte Rhys Boardman arrived in February 2016. Charlotte is also here to bring joy and happiness to the family, around Carole's anniversary.

Carole is so proud of her growing family and is proud of what a wonderful grandfather her gorgeous husband John is. Carole wants John to know that he is doing a wonderful job of looking after their girls and keeping Carole's memory alive.

Her last message to John is that he is her 'Endless love – and until we meet again!'

* * *

Message from John:
2004 – My first encounter with Debbie was sometime in 2004 at our shop in Gymea – as a customer. On leaving our shop Debbie began talking with the lady from the shop next door and I was somehow curious to find out who she was.

I was told that Debbie worked from her home and she was a psychic medium, which didn't mean much to me at that time.

Fast forward to 2011 – My beautiful wife Carole passed away in February of that year from cancer. My son's mother-in-law, Alison, insisted that I should see a psychic to help me with my loss. At the time I said, 'No'. But after a few months of gentle reminders I said that I would look into it. After doing a Google search, Debbie Malone's name came up so I gave her a call to make an appointment.

I was told that I could have an appointment the very next day at 9.30 a.m. Upon meeting Debbie I said: 'You're the lady who I saw in our shop in Gymea in 2004!' How strange I thought to myself.

From that moment on my life changed. My reading with Debbie was a beautiful and uplifting experience that has given me so much peace and understanding of the afterlife. I know that Carole is always with me and I no longer feel guilty about living while she is in spirit.

I know that when I am experiencing happiness and joy with the children that she is also feeling that same feeling. I am now living for both of us and I know that we will be together again one day. I know the love we shared will always be between us. I can see her memory kept alive in our children and grandchildren and this gives me a purpose for my time here. I am no longer a skeptic – I believe!

Regards,
John Boardman

CHAPTER 5

Signs From Above

Robert Malone, my gorgeous father-in-law, passed in 2012, of pancreatic cancer; this was a tremendous loss to our family. Robert ('Bob' or 'Pop' as we called him) Malone was an extraordinary man with great knowledge and insight. He was a wonderful husband, father and grandfather, who always had time for his family, friends and, most of all, his grandchildren.

This chapter is about some of the wonderful insights Bob has passed on to his family from this life, and the next. To be honest, there are so many wonderful things about Bob, I could write a whole book about him. The most important thing I wish to share with you during this chapter, however, is that our loved ones go to great lengths to give us signs from above.

Bob was born in Sydney and, at the age of six, moved with his family to live in Werris Creek, NSW. Bob's father was away working in Papua New Guinea during this time, to support the family, managing a copra plantation.

Bob loved to go exploring in the bush. He would go rabbit shooting with his older brother Ken, on Mount Terrible, which was known to the locals as 'Terrible Billy'. Bob and his brother would sell the rabbit pelts to help support the family while their father was in Papua New Guinea.

On one of their rabbit shooting trips Bob found a baby magpie that had fallen from its nest. Bob wrapped the baby bird in his hat and brought it home to be hand-raised. He named the baby magpie 'Jacko'.

Robert (Bob) "Poppy" and Enid Malone

The only problem was that Jacko didn't know he was a magpie and he took on the role as the family's watchdog.

Bob always had a love for animals and nature. Bob absolutely loved his new-found friend and he promptly taught him to talk.

On his father's return to Australia the family moved to Kingsgrove, when Bob was in his early teens. Jacko made the big move to Sydney with the family.

Jacko wasn't kept in a cage like other pet birds; he lived under the family home. He would perch himself on the gas pipe that led from the side of the house to underneath the floorboards.

As the foundations of the house were elevated, about 1 metre off the ground, there was enough room for Jacko to comfortably sit and watch the comings and goings of family and friends.

When anyone would enter the driveway and pass Jacko's perch he would call out to the family, saying: 'Mum, Mum'. This was to alert them that someone was approaching. Jacko lived to a ripe old age and so the story began of this very special bird.

* * *

When my three children were little, Bob, 'Pop', relayed the adventures of Jacko, the talking Magpie, to them. Whenever the children stayed over at Pop and Grandma's house they would ask Bob to tell them the story.

I wonder if Bob ever became sick of relaying the same tale over and over again (it wasn't until Bob's passing that we all truly understood the importance of Jacko)?

Every time my children saw a magpie at Pop's house, or in our backyard, they would become very excited and shout out that Jacko had come to visit them. From that time on, any magpie in close proximity to my children was then nick-named Jacko.

* * *

Bob had always been a very fit and healthy man, who prided himself on being an integral part of his family. He always looked on the bright side and he never complained about anything in life.

In 2011, I began to notice a change in Bob and I became concerned about his health. As Bob got older he developed skin cancers on his arms and legs. Bob was regularly treated by a skin specialist and had multiple skin cancers cut out or burnt off his legs and arms. I spoke to Bob about the concerns I had for his health, but he just smiled and told me that he was all right. Deep down, though, I knew he wasn't all right! I worried that he was already, or about to become, unwell.

I asked him about his health and suggested that he should have a full checkup at the doctor, not just the skin specialist. Bob just smiled and said: 'I'm all right!' But the messages I was receiving from spirit were telling me that, due to the multiple surgeries on his legs to remove the skin cancers, the cancer had gotten into his bloodstream and spread.

Bob began to have issues with his stomach and at first the doctors thought he had a stomach ulcer. He had numerous blood tests, which all came back clear. It wasn't until further investigations were done that my worst fears came to fruition. Bob was diagnosed with pancreatic cancer in February 2012. It was a huge shock to all of the family when Bob gave us the bad news. I felt very upset with myself that I didn't push him further to see another doctor, concerning the skin cancers.

Bob was told that there was nothing further, medically, that could be done to save him. The doctor's first advised him against having chemotherapy because they didn't think it would assist his situation. He was then advised that it might prolong his life, so he began his chemotherapy treatment. I begged him not to have it as I could see it was going to make him pass sooner. Which was what ultimately happened.

Bob's life became a never-ending list of doctor's appointments, treatments and then, finally, trips to hospital. Warwick, my husband, the children and I, would visit him each afternoon and try to keep his spirits up. I would talk to him about his life when he was growing up. We spoke about Jacko and I finally had the courage to ask him about giving us a sign when he transitioned into the spirit world.

Even though I am a medium it is still very hard to speak to a treasured loved one about giving you signs when they die. (It is hard to even say the word 'die'; we tend to say 'pass away', 'cross over', 'transition' or 'reach the other side'.) We never talk about death, we talk about birth, life and living. How ironic, though, because from the moment we are born we know deep down that we are going to die. Yet this is something none of us ever wants to discuss, let alone think about and face. I guess in some ways I am fortunate to have experienced so many near-death experiences, which have given me insight into the fact that when we 'die' or transition, our soul lives on and begins another form of life. The hardest part of this knowledge is that we all need to go through this experience to understand it is a reality.

* * *

Prior to starting his chemotherapy treatment, Bob was still quite active and was able to manage his pain, but I could see the light and life die within him. I tried to get him to make a bucket list so that we could attempt to give him goals to look forward to. However, it was too late – the cancer was now in control and it was only a matter of time before he would lose his battle with the dreadful disease.

The year of his passing was also a year of milestones for my children, his grandchildren. Unfortunately, due to his illness and his deterioration, he was not able to attend Blake's eighteenth or Shannon's sixteenth birthdays, which was a great blow to him and, of course, to his loving grandchildren. This is something we will never forget, as Pop was always a part of all of the children's milestones in life and he was greatly missed on these occasions.

Although he didn't get to do the few things he had written on his bucket list, my husband, children and I have decided that we will try to do them on his behalf, with Grandma. He had once worked on the trains and he loved them. He also wanted to be well enough to come to Blake's eighteenth and Shannon's sixteenth birthday parties. He also spoke about going on a cruise from Sydney to Melbourne for the Melbourne Cup, if he was still alive in November. November was a very important time for him as it is his son, Warwick's, and his wife, Enid's, birthday month.

Unfortunately, Pop wasn't alive long enough to go on the Melbourne Cup cruise. However, Shannon, Warwick, Enid and I did book and go.

Even though Pop didn't come with us, in life, on the cruise, we knew that he was with us in spirit. Grandma had an amazing time on the cruise and we were all quite lucky at the races that day. We even saw a magpie at the racecourse, which let us all know that Pop was with us.

* * *

Prior to Pop's deterioration he wished to be able to pass at home amongst the family. However, due to the pain and suffering he was experiencing with the cancer, he was admitted to hospital. He was firstly admitted to Sutherland Hospital, in the palliative care ward, located in Miranda. This was the beginning of the end. Due to the funding issues that our public hospitals were experiencing at the time (and I am sure they still experience today) Pop suffered greatly. Due to a lack of beds, mental patients were admitted into the ward he was staying in.

My poor father-in-law was terrified to go to sleep as one such patient would try to pull him out of bed or try and steal his clothes or personal items. The nurses were at a loss as to how they could manage this man. We did all we could for Pop and he was finally allowed to go home and find a little peace and quiet.

Pop was at home for a few weeks before he underwent another round of chemotherapy. People say that chemotherapy saves people, and I am sure in many cases it does. However, when you are 83 years of age and there is no cure, why would the medical fraternity subject someone to such pain and anguish? Why is it not recommended that a terminally ill loved one be given pain management and quality of life instead of being offered poison that costs a lot of money, causes you pain and suffering, and inevitably kills you anyway.

Unfortunately it was only a short time before Pop was re-admitted to hospital. However it was to the Calvary Hospital, in Kogarah, which was once a hospital for only the terminally ill. To this day many of us remember that this was the hospital that many loved ones would never return from.

When we would go to visit Pop he would just ask us when he was going to go home. It was so difficult to see his frustration at being in a place he knew he may never return from. Even though Pop was a private patient, there were not enough private rooms at the hospital, so he had to share a room with three other patients, only separated by a retractable curtain.

The feeling of depression in the room was dreadful. Across from Pop was a young man in his early forties in the last stages of cancer. He looked like a withered old man, even though he was very young. One day we went in to see Pop and we asked him where the man had gone. Pop solemnly replied that he was in another room and we later heard that he had passed.

* * *

Blake and I went to visit Pop. I explained to Pop that I was going to Adelaide early the next morning to appear at the Body, Mind and Psychic Expo. I would be staying overnight and returning to Sydney on Sunday. I told Pop that I would come to see him on the way back from the airport. I asked Pop how he was feeling and he replied: 'Not much good could come from this; the worst is yet to come!' I will never forget his words; they still ring in my ears.

Pop didn't really indicate how sick he truly was during our visit. He was actually looking better than he had in the last few weeks. We chatted about Blake's work and his paintings. With a blue pen, Pop started to draw the scene he could see from his hospital bed, onto a notepad, for Blake. Then a nurse came to take him away to have an ultrasound, so we both hugged him and gave him a kiss goodbye. If only I had realised that this would be the last time that I would see him conscious, I would have, and should have, said so much more to him. This has been something that has haunted me since his passing.

I flew over to Adelaide the following morning and appeared at the show. When I finished, I rang Warwick to see how Pop was. He said that he was okay. However, that night Pop took a turn for the worse. I remember going to bed and I couldn't stop thinking of him. I tried to sleep but I felt like I was drowning. I began to cough uncontrollably and I felt extremely unwell. Warwick rang me a few moments later and said that his father was having problems breathing and I knew that I had been picking up on what he was experiencing. I struggled to go to sleep and I was so worried. I could feel Pop's pain. I felt helpless that I was so far away and couldn't be of more assistance to Warwick and the family.

Warwick rang me early in the morning and said that the family were all going to the hospital because Pop had deteriorated rapidly overnight. I cancelled the other event I was booked in for at the Expo and got on to the first plane to Sydney. All I could think of was not being back in time to see Pop before he passed away.

The flight felt like the longest flight ever. At approximately 11.20 a.m. I began to hear Pop talking to me in the same way as I communicate with those in spirit. I could hear him loud and clear and he was telling me not to worry, that it was all right. I began to sob silently to myself because I felt that this meant that he had died while I was still on my way to see him. The lady sitting beside me on the plane tapped me on the shoulder and asked me if I was okay. When I explained to her that I was trying to make it home to see my father-in-law before he passed, she gave me a big hug to comfort me.

Unbeknownst to me, back in Sydney Pop had been calling out for me and kept asking where I was at the same time I could hear him while I was on the plane. A short time later the minister came to visit Pop and give him his last rites.

The plane finally landed at the airport and I was able to turn my phone back on. I rang Warwick and he confirmed that his father was still alive, although it didn't seem as if he had much time left. I asked him to tell his dad that I was on my way and I would be with him soon. My only hope was that I made it in time.

The cab driver was amazing – he seemed to fly to the hospital and we made it there in record time. When I entered I realised that Pop had been moved to his own room. Such a shame that he had to be so close to death to receive the dignity he so rightly deserved.

All of the family were gathered around Pop's bed when I walked in. The solemn desperation I could feel was overwhelming. I went and stood by Pop's side and I told him that I was there. He very slightly squeezed my hand in acknowledgement that he knew that I was there. I told him how much I loved him and then I began to hear him speaking with me again like he had on the plane.

All of the contact I had from this point onwards was telepathic. Pop never regained consciousness, although we were constantly communicating until he died.

The hardest thing for me to accept was how angry I was with myself for not picking up on how unwell he was. I berated myself that if I was properly tuned in as a psychic/medium, then how could I not have known how sick Pop was. I questioned myself about why I even went to the Expo when I could have had more precious time with him before he died. To this day I ask myself these questions, over and over again. Yes, I know that everything happens for a reason, but at challenging times in our lives we question what that reason is.

Warwick confirmed that at the time I began to hear his father speaking to me on the flight home, it was the exact time his father was calling out for me. Only moments later he was being administered his last rites. I then realised how privileged I was to have been given such an amazing opportunity to communicate with him, and also to know that Pop was waiting for me to come before he left this Earthly plane.

All the family sat with Pop for what seemed like an eternity. Everyone sat there solemnly waiting for the inevitable. I felt that this was the time I needed to verbalise everything I wish I had said and also to see what Pop could do to show us that when it was time for him to transition, he would give us signs from above. As I write this I look back at this time and realise that it was precious; it was irreplaceable and unmeasurable and I can't thank him enough for what he shared with us all.

I spoke to Pop about giving us all messages, in the form of magpies, from the spirit world. I asked him to show himself as a magpie, like his beloved pet magpie Jacko. Telepathically, Pop promised that he would go to great lengths to return in this form to all of the family. I promised him that I would always look after Grandma, and I told her she was in safe hands. I also asked him what he wanted done during his funeral and he asked me if I could help to organise the event so that Grandma didn't need to worry. I promised him that he didn't need to worry; everything would be organised and taken care of. He was most worried about the paperwork (Pop had always taken care of everything for his beautiful soulmate).

As the energy in the room became heavier and the sadness grew, I clearly heard Pop tell me that it was time for me to take the children home. He didn't want to die in front of them. Now, this was one of the hardest things for me to do because none of us wanted to leave his side. I asked him if he would change his mind – we wanted to be there until the end.

Once again I heard him say it was time to go and he promised me that he would let me know when he had left Earth. I re-affirmed to him before I left him, that no matter what happened, I would always look after my mother-in-law, my children's beautiful grandma. I told him that if there were any messages he wanted to pass on to the rest of the family, he knew what to do. Pop was very well aware of what I do, so he knew exactly where to come to get a message across.

As you can imagine this was an extremely hard thing to do. I did not want to let my children down or take my children away from their beautiful Pop and I also did not want to delay his transition and prolong his pain. I dutifully drove my children home in the car. We all sat silently on the drive, with tears streaming down our faces.

When we arrived home we all tried to go to sleep, knowing deep down inside that when we woke up the world would be missing an amazing soul and the spirit world would be gaining an amazing angel. My husband had stayed behind at the hospital to be with his brother, sister and their mother.

I was very restless during the night and felt great guilt for not staying behind. However, as a mother I did not want my children to grieve alone.

Pop had promised that he would let me know when he transitioned into the spirit world. There was a little joke that Pop and I shared for many years. My children played hockey when they were little, and into their teens, and they were chosen to play representative hockey for Sydney. During winter, Grandma and Pop would usually come and stay with us when we went to the country competitions and State Championships. Pop was always someone who would wake up early in the morning, even if the rest of us didn't. Sometimes if we went away we would share a family room or cabin at the location where the children were playing. Pop thought it was always a bit of fun to come and knock on the bedside table or the wall beside my head: tap, tap, tap, silence, tap, tap, tap, and then ask me if I was awake yet. Sometimes it would really annoy me when he would do this at 5 a.m. or 6 a.m. in the morning, especially after having a late night at a cold hockey field. After waking me up, he would always ask me, with a very cheeky smile, if I would like a cup of tea. When I saw that smile, how on earth could I be cranky with him, even if he had woken me up? To be honest, I wish that he could still do this 1000 more times, just so I could see his cheeky, smiling face and have him here with us now.

Early in the morning he came and told me that he had passed. I was woken up with the familiar tapping: tap, tap, tap, silence, tap, tap, tap, beside my head. I immediately woke up and was about to ring Warwick when the phone rang. I picked it up and of course Warwick was on the end of the line giving me the extremely sad, yet expected, news that Pop had transitioned into the spirit world. Then I woke the children up and with a heavy heart told them that Pop had passed away. We were all in a daze and found it hard to concentrate on what we had to do next.

Once we were all dressed, I drove to the hospital. I remember that the sun was just beginning to rise and there wasn't much traffic on the road.

The sky was beautiful with the muted colours of the sunrise, however our spirits felt dark and grey inside. The feeling was so surreal as we drove. We all knew that, from this time forward, our lives would never be the same.

I parked the car close to the hospital and caught the front of my car on the kerb. I heard the loud scraping sound and thought that this was the beginning of a very less-than-perfect day. To be honest, I don't know what I was thinking at all. I just wanted this day to end. If I could have turned back time and brought Pop back, then I would have done anything I could to make this wish come true. But I knew this was the end, and the beginning of a new life without a very special family member. The hardest part was working out how to take the next step forward.

We walked into Pop's room. Everyone present had tears streaming down their faces. To be honest, I have never seen a dead person in real life before. I have worked on many, many murder investigations, but have never come face-to-face with death.

Here I was staring at someone I loved dearly. Death was not what I thought it would be. It was a feeling of peacefulness and contentment. My beautiful father-in-law looked so at peace. He looked very relaxed and content; he just looked as if he was in a deep sleep. He still had colour in his face and all of the pain I had seen during the last few months had disappeared. He looked extremely well, better than I had seen him for some months. It saddened me to know that 'no', he wasn't asleep, and 'yes' he had gone to the other side.

We all sat with Pop for a few last precious moments. We all told him how much we loved him and how much we would miss him. Each of us talked about what an amazing man he was. I could see Pop in spirit, standing in the room making sure we were all okay. He wanted to ensure, before leaving this Earth, that we would all cope without his beautiful soul being present in our lives. The most important thing I wanted to tell him was what a great gift it was to have had him in our lives.

After our farewell, I returned home with the family and sprang into action. I was so lucky to hear Pop in my ear telling me what he wanted me to do along the way. I had to go to Officeworks to pick up some items for the funeral. However, when I was driving past a plant nursery on the way home, Pop told me how important it was for me to stop and buy something for Grandma.

Grandma absolutely loves gardening, which all of the family are well aware of. Pop told me that it was extremely important to look for a plant that would show his love for her. I was so brain dead I didn't know what to look for. I suddenly felt Pop's energy by my side and he guided me over to a large selection of roses. He wanted me to pick roses with names that captured their enduring love. The roses Pop helped me to choose were named 'Truly Yours' and 'Remember Me'; then he guided me to the pot section and helped me to choose two pots for her.

I promptly took the roses home and potted them up for Grandma and placed them on her back porch. The roses were in a dormant state when I bought them, but it only took a couple of weeks for them to come back to life and promptly grow new shoots. Shortly after this, both of the rose plants began to bud. This was quite unusual as it was not the time of year when roses usually flower. We all knew that Pop had something to do with this. When the flowers opened they were huge and their fragrance was very strong like roses used to be. Now, each year, Pop delivers Grandma messages of his love through the two rose plants I bought for her on the day of his passing. Each year Pop sends roses to remind Grandma that he was 'Truly Yours' and wants her to 'Remember Me'.

This is the message on the tag on the rose plant called 'Remember Me', which Pop guided me to: *Remember me in your heart, your thoughts and your memories. The times we loved. The times we cried. The times we laughed and the times we shared together will always be remembered!*

* * *

As Pop was the patriarch of the family it was hard to think of what we all needed to do next. The one thing that Pop was adamant about was that the funeral be arranged by Olsen's Funerals at Sutherland. Pop played bowls for both the Gymea and Sutherland bowling clubs and Olsen's sponsored some of the special bowling club days. Out of loyalty, Pop wanted them to be the ones to arrange his funeral.

There was one problem, however. The family felt we had to use the chapel at Sutherland, for the service. The chapel is extremely small and not all of Pop's family and friends would have been able to fit inside. A close friend of our father had his funeral at that chapel and I became extremely unwell during the service and had to leave. This was due to the heavy energy and amount of spirits there. I felt so unwell that it took me a few days to recover, so I hoped I could change the family's mind to have the funeral at the Woronora Cemetery chapel instead. The energy was light and uplifting, there, and it was big enough to accommodate all those who wished to attend.

I rang Olsen's and asked if they could conduct the funeral at Woronora Cemetery chapel as an alternative, and they said it wasn't an issue as long as all of the family agreed. Thankfully, the family understood and the funeral was organised to be held at Woronora instead.

The few days leading up to the funeral were very hectic and a blur. I did the artwork for Pop's memorial-service booklet. My daughter, Shannon, and I organised the slideshow for the funeral as well as the music. This sounds like a small task until you realise how many photographs you need to go through. Finding the right words, verses, and deciding what photographs should be included within a 4–5 minute slideshow depicting 83 precious years of Pop's life, was quite confronting. The most important thing was to honour what he wanted.

There were three significant songs we used in the slideshow. These were 'Close To You' by The Carpenters, 'The Blue Danube' by Johann Strauss and 'On My Way Home' by Enya. It was amazing how these three songs would suddenly start to play in obscure places after the funeral.

The hardest challenge was to find photographs of Pop during the different times in his life. As Pop was always the photographer and not in front of the camera, there were periods in his life that were missing. Since discovering this challenge, I have reminded all of the family just how important photographs truly are to those left behind.

During the three days prior to the funeral, Pop made his presence known to me via clairaudience as well as magpie visits and rainbows. From the day Pop died and until his funeral, the weather was bleak, raining and grey. I felt that this was an extension of how we were all feeling while coping with our loss.

On the Tuesday after Pop's passing I visited Westfield Miranda Fair in South Sydney, to try to purchase the paper that I wanted to use for the memorial booklets. Thinking about the whole situation on the way back to the car, I felt very overwhelmed and I broke down. My car was parked in the open-roof car park area at Miranda, facing Pop's house. As I returned to the car a magnificent half-rainbow appeared from out of the gloomy sky. The rainbow finished right on top of his house, brightening it up with brilliant rainbow-coloured light. This immediately put a smile back on my face. I knew that this was a sign from above. I also felt that it meant that he was sharing light with Grandma. (Whenever I see a rainbow I feel complete-and-utter joy. I don't feel the end of the rainbow is where the pot of gold will be found; instead, I know that this is the bridge to allow our loved ones to come down from Heaven to reunite with us here on Earth. This rainbow certainly signified this to me.)

After leaving Miranda I stopped in at Grandma's house to check on her and to see if there was anything I could do for her. As I parked the car in the driveway a magpie landed in front of me and walked down the driveway ahead of me. The magpie jumped through the wrought-iron gates and casually walked on down to the backyard.

I rang the doorbell and told Grandma about our special visitor. We went through the house and looked out into the backyard and, sure enough, there was the magpie just standing in the backyard, looking up at us. I told Grandma that this was a sign that Pop was all right. This was just the beginning of our magpie visits.

On returning home, a magpie landed on the roof of our house and sat there for over an hour, singing quite contently. Warwick was still a bit of a skeptic even after all of the experiences our family had gone through. However, even he had to admit that this was a message from his father.

* * *

The week of the funeral was also the beginning of the 2012 Mind, Body and Spirit festival in Melbourne. As well as organising the funeral I still had to go to Melbourne due to my prior commitments – I was not able to cancel. The festival is a four-day event. I usually fly down a day in advance to set up for the festival and then I fly out the day after it finishes. The festival set-up was on the Thursday and the first day of the festival was on the Friday, which was the same day as the funeral. It appeared I would have to fly to Melbourne immediately after the funeral, on a 5 p.m. flight.

The Tuesday before the funeral I was up at my office, feeling overwhelmed and worried if I was doing the right thing with the arrangements to go to Melbourne.

I lay down on my office lounge and began to cry uncontrollably, overwhelmed by grief. Suddenly, I felt the energy in my office change and the room became extremely cold. A little voice popped into my head and said: 'Don't worry, Deb, it will be all right!' I then felt a gentle hand pat me on my leg, as a sign of comfort. I knew that this was Pop reassuring me everything would work out okay. I opened my teary eyes and I looked down at my leg where I had felt the comforting pat. To my surprise there was a little white feather there on my black jeans.

That afternoon my manager came to my office to help me pack everything to take to Melbourne. As we were discussing the festival and I spoke about hoping that I was doing the right thing, the fans in my office suddenly all turned themselves on to high speed. The fans can only be turned on via the remote and, as we were both sitting on the floor packing the boxes, we turned to each other and I said: 'I think this is a sign to go.'

Three days later was the day of the funeral. We parked the car and began to walk to Woronora Crematorium chapel. A magpie landed just in front of us on the roadway and walked with us to the chapel. I told Warwick that I always knew that Pop would want to come to his own funeral, to make sure that Grandma was all right, not to mention I am sure he wanted to reunite with all his friends and family one last time.

I arrived early on the morning of the funeral at the Crematorium to do a check that the slideshow would work and unfortunately, the music would not sync up. However, at the vital time of the funeral everything went to plan. Pop was in attendance and I could see he was happy. That was all I could have wished for.

When the funeral ended I briefly attended the wake before flying to Melbourne. This was such a challenge as I felt I was deserting the family in their time of need. But, unfortunately, I had no choice.

Shannon and I arrived in Melbourne, virtually shell-shocked. That night we both sat in our hotel room hugging and comforting each other. While we were watching television, the Carpenters' song 'Close To You' began to play in the background of a television show we were watching. Then an advertisement came on a few minutes later and the backing track was the 'The Blue Danube'. This confirmed to us that Pop was by our sides.

The next day I knew that I had to put on a happy face. For the next three days I assisted and comforted others who were experiencing grief and loss, as I also quietly suffered in silence. When I arrived at my stand, my manager had thoughtfully arranged to have a sign put up the day before to explain why I hadn't been at my stand. It read: 'Due to unforeseen circumstances Debbie will not be available to do readings today.' My manager is such a wonderful person in my life and he always has my best interests at heart. I totally understand that he was trying to protect me, but unfortunately this backfired. If he had put, 'Due to a death in the family Debbie is not available to do readings today', people would have been more understanding. A journalist from one of the Melbourne papers had a field day in their column, writing that 'if I was so psychic then I should have seen the unforeseen circumstances.' Yes, so funny, but not under the circumstances I was experiencing.

So, as you can imagine, I was the laughing-stock of the Melbourne psychic scene for a couple of days. Pity the journalist who wrote the story wasn't more understanding. When I contacted the paper they said it was my fault for putting up the sign in the first place. I had many people coming to my stand pointing out the story, which really didn't help with my grief.

While I was at the Mind, Body and Spirit festival another gifted medium came to visit me on my stand. He was not aware of why I had been a day late attending the festival. He came up and gave me a hug and asked if I was okay. He then proceeded to give me a message. He asked if I had lost a fatherly energy, and I answered: 'Yes'. He then said: 'I have a man here who is showing me that when he was younger he lived in a rural location.' He said that this man felt like a father or father-in-law and he wanted me to know that he is okay. He then said not to worry as the male energy was with me and guiding me over the weekend and that everything would be good. He then went on to describe what my father-in-law looked like and the type of personality he had.

I am a very private person and this man gave me some much-needed reassurance. I was very emotional after this. It took me a few moments to compose myself and truly appreciate that the work we do as psychic mediums can be of such huge significance.

* * *

These messages thankfully assisted me to be able to cope with the readings and workshops over the next three days. One of the readings on the first day of the festival was for a lady who had recently lost her father due to pancreatic cancer. This has to have been one of the most confronting readings I did during the weekend. As you can imagine, all of the past few months came flooding back into my head.

The client's recent experiences mirrored what my family had just gone through. Her father had also suffered with chemotherapy in the same manner that my father-in-law had. I felt as if I was looking into a mirror. It is interesting to note that, as a medium, your life reflects back when you are doing readings for others. I feel that if you aren't empathetic to others then you aren't able to relate to others' needs. You learn that you are not only connecting with others and assisting them with their grief, but you are also connecting with your higher self and, in some form, connecting to spirit and healing within yourself.

This particular weekend was an overwhelming challenge. I was extremely open and able to connect with the beautiful clients I met during the festival. The workshops I held also connected me to those who were in loss. I felt that Pop was with me every step of the way to help me cope, and to guide and assist the wonderful people I met during that weekend.

* * *

Since overcoming the loss of Pop, the messages and signs he has been sharing have not stopped. Pop was true to his word that he would make his presence known every way he could.

Blake is an artist, and while he was finishing Year 12 he was chosen for ArtExpress, which is an exhibition created by high-school students during their Higher School Certificate Examination in Visual Arts. The government liked his artworks so much that they purchased his entire collection to be part of the Wilkins Collection. Part of being chosen to be in ArtExpress was that his collection was to also be exhibited at Moree Plains Gallery in August 2012. This was a major breakthrough in Blake's life.

The opening night took place a little over a month after Pop's passing. This was to be the first major family event without him. Pop and Grandma were always with us during all of the children's major events, so it was quite emotional not to have him with us. Of course Grandma came to the opening.

We set off on the trip to Moree. It reminded us all of one of the National Lampoon vacation movies. My husband said that the trip would only take 5–6 hours when in fact it took nearly ten hours, including stopovers. Warwick and I took turns with the driving. During the entire trip, magpies would be sitting along the side of the road as we passed. We all laughed and said that Pop was keeping an eye on us.

In the afternoon, we stopped at one of the roadside rest areas. As I was driving out of the car park area hundreds of white feathers floated in front of the car and covered the bonnet and windscreen. I knew I hadn't hit a bird but I stopped the car to check that everything was all right. Of course there was no bird to be seen, just an amazing display of white feathers floating down onto our car. I took this as a sign from above that someone was trying to get my attention.

The light started to fade as the sun began to set behind the trees. The magpies I had seen earlier seemed to be appearing more and more often than they had during the whole trip. I made a comment that Pop was really trying to get our attention. Suddenly, I heard him say, as clear as a bell, in my ear: 'Slow down! There is a kangaroo up ahead!'

I decelerated and told Warwick what his father had said to me. Suddenly, on the left-hand side of the car a big grey kangaroo came bounding out of the bush and stopped on the side of the road.

I slowed down even more in case it jumped in front of the car. Thankfully I passed it without any incident, and then another magpie appeared. I said to Warwick: 'See – I told you your dad was warning me about the kangaroo!' Warwick just looked at me and shook his head.

We attended the exhibition opening at the art gallery the following day. During the entire time we were at Moree, magpies appeared from nowhere, giving us all comforting signs that Pop was not far away.

* * *

On our return, Pop's ashes were ready to be picked up from the crematorium. My mother-in-law and sister-in-law went to collect them, as well as choosing a place for his ashes to be interred. When they parked the car and started to walk to the office, a magpie landed near them and followed them all the way to the office and back. Because Pop came from the country and loved nature, Pop's ashes were placed in the native bush garden. When they walked to the area to pick out the niche to place his ashes and plaque, the magpie continued to walk with them. It then sat close by when they made their decision.

When Grandma arrived home she couldn't wait to tell us that Pop had been with her, helping her to choose the place where he would like to be interred.

* * *

Every Tuesday night Pop would come to visit after he took Grandma to her line-dancing class. This was an extremely special time for us as he would tell us stories about his life and he would always help the children with their homework. Pop had been an engineer and he was very gifted with maths. Pop would spend many hours with my daughter helping her to do her Year 11 maths homework. After he passed she found it challenging to do her maths without his assistance. It wasn't the fact that she couldn't do the homework alone, it was more the fact that this was her special time together with Pop.

The following year, after Pop had passed, Shannon had her Year 12 maths exams. On this particular morning she was very quiet, which is unusual for her. While we were sitting having breakfast prior to leaving for school, I asked her what was wrong and she burst into tears. She said that she was very nervous about her exams and she wished that Pop were still here to help her. I said to her that she didn't have to worry – Pop was only a thought away. I told her that all she had to do was think of him and ask for his assistance and he would be there. Just as I said this, a magpie landed on the table right outside the kitchen's glass sliding door. The magpie sat there looking straight at Shannon, moving its head from side to side as if to communicate with her. We both laughed and she said: 'I think that this means that Pop will help me with my maths exam today.'

When Shannon arrived home from her exam I asked her how she went. She said that she felt that she went really well. She then relayed that when she felt that she was stuck answering a question, she could feel Pop was with her and the answer would pop into her head.

Well, I am happy to report that Pop must have truly been there with her on the day of her exams. When she received her Higher School Certificate results, she had passed her maths exams with flying colours, thanks to Pop.

* * *

Our dog, Sonny, was also extremely fond of Pop. Whenever Grandma came to visit after Pop had passed, Sonny would be waiting for Pop, too. He would run around the house looking for him, wondering where he was. Also since Pop's passing, a magpie frequently comes to the back door and sits and looks into our house. This magpie is very cheeky.

He will play games with Sonny, by swooping down and pinching his dog biscuits. Other times the magpie will sit on the back deck or on the bird feeder. This magpie is very tame and can be hand fed. He also loves to sing his beautiful serenade.

* * *

On the first anniversary of Pop's passing, the family went to visit him at the cemetery. We had an idea of where his plaque was in the native bush garden, but we weren't exactly sure of the location. It didn't take us long to find it, though. When we went into the section of the garden we saw a magpie sitting up in a tree directly above the spot. The magpie was looking directly at us, singing away very happily. It was as though he had been waiting for us to arrive and he was singing to us as a way of welcoming us to the spot. We all looked at each other and smiled. Yes, Pop was truly with us.

* * *

In July 2014, I was staying in Melbourne for a weekend to run some workshops. As we had a spare day, Shannon and I decided it would be a good opportunity to tick off one of our bucket-list goals. We booked a bus tour going to the Twelve Apostles at Port Campbell and also a helicopter flight over the area. Due to our early pick-up time, we hadn't watched the news that morning. It was only while we were travelling down to Port Campbell that we heard that the Malaysian Airlines flight MH17 had been shot down over the Ukraine. This news marred the trip down as a sombre occasion instead of an exciting one.

*Poppy gives us a sign from above. A magpie appeared just
before our helicopter trip at the Twelve Apostles, Victoria*

On the way to our destination the weather was appalling. It was
raining heavily, the winds were extremely strong and it was freezing
cold. I just hoped that the weather would improve when we finally
arrived at the Twelve Apostles. The news of the plane crash was still
fresh in my mind.

During the trip we stopped at points of interest along the way and
Shannon and I discussed whether or not we felt it was safe enough to do
the helicopter flight.

When we finally arrived at the heliport, there was a huge line of people ahead of us. We stood there patiently, waiting for our flight. The longer we waited the more nervous I became. I am extremely frightened of heights; Shannon, on the other hand, is a very brave young lady. Not much bothers her. I just hoped that the wind would settle down and that our flight wouldn't end in disaster. I know that this doesn't sound at all rational; however, it always seems that air crashes come in threes and we didn't want to be one of them.

Suddenly, a magpie landed on the tarmac just in front of where we were standing. It was incredible that the magpie was even able to do this with the turbulence from the landings and take-offs of the three helicopters. The magpie just sat in front of us looking at us quite calmly. We both knew that this was another sign from Pop, telling us both that everything was going to be all right.

We had to wait in the line another twenty minutes before it was our turn to fly. The magpie wandered around on the tarmac in front of us until our helicopter left. As we flew over the majestic Twelve Apostles, the sun broke through and a double rainbow appeared in front of us. As we flew towards the rainbows our helicopter was encircled in the complete, circular rainbow. The pilot said that during all of the years of flying helicopters he had never experienced anything like this before. Shannon and I knew that Pop had been pretty busy orchestrating such a beautiful, breathtaking event. The flight seemed to end quickly, however the sight of the beautiful circular rainbow is something Shannon and I will never forget.

* * *

In August 2014 I had a vision of my husband getting a new ute. His car at the time was blue, but in my vision the ute I saw him driving was bright and shiny white. When I arrived home from work

I asked him if he was thinking of buying a new ute. He just looked at me and replied: 'No, there is nothing wrong with the one I have.' I explained to him that I had a vision of him with a white ute.

Three weeks later I was at work conducting readings when the phone rang. When I am doing readings I don't answer the phone because it interrupts the flow of the reading and is rude to the client. But on this particular day the phone rang constantly. Then my mobile started to ring. Warwick's face suddenly popped into my head and I explained to the client that I felt I needed to answer the phone as I felt that something was wrong.

When I answered the phone Warwick told me that he had been in a head-on car accident. He explained that a woman had gone through a red light when he was turning with a green arrow. The woman hit his car so hard that his car was a write-off. Thankfully he was only bruised and shaken. He asked me if I could come down to help him get all of his tools out of the car as it had been towed to a smash repair. I promptly rang my manager and asked him to reschedule the rest of my readings for that day. I drove down to the smash-repair shop at Taren Point. The location of the smash repair is extremely busy, with vehicles constantly driving past. I was lucky to find a parking space out the front.

When I looked at the damage to the car I couldn't believe that Warwick was even alive. Suddenly, a magpie flew down right beside where we were standing. I am sure it was Pop, and I am sure that the vision I had was one my beautiful father-in-law shared with me in order for me to know that Warwick was going to be in safe hands.

* * *

A few weeks later Warwick received the all clear from the insurance company to buy another car. It took him some time to find exactly the type of car he wanted. He went to visit a car yard in the hope that he might purchase a black ute that he had seen advertised. When he arrived, however, he found one that was more suitable – and it was white. When he drove into the driveway with his new car, I just smiled and said: 'I told you that you were getting a new white ute!' He then said: 'Why didn't you see that I was going to be in a car accident?' I replied: 'All I saw in my vision was that you were driving a new, shiny white ute and you were alive and well.'

* * *

After the accident, we were booked to go on a cruise to New Zealand for two weeks. Unfortunately, on the day we were meant to leave, the cruise was cancelled due to mechanical issues with the ship. This left our holiday plans in disarray. Due to the late notice, it was impossible to organise a holiday on the dates that we were available to travel. At the last minute I decided to book a week away at Port Stephens.

Part of the reason we were going on the cruise was to tick more off the bucket list. Fortunately, two of the things on the list were also possible at Port Stephens.

One of those things was to quad bike on sand dunes, which was possible at Stockton Beach. We drove to the Stockton Beach meeting point and were met by the quad-bike instructor. We were all kitted up for the bike ride and were driven out to the dunes.

Warwick and I were very fortunate to be the only two people on our tour. We were instructed on how to ride the bike and then we were off. What an amazing experience we had. Our guide started us off by taking us across smaller dunes and then building up to bigger ones. As we progressed along the sand dunes we saw a very familiar sight. Guess who was with us? In the middle of a huge sand dune with nothing but sand surrounding him, was a lone magpie, sitting waiting for us. A little further ahead another magpie landed.

I called out to Warwick and pointed to our familiar friends. Warwick said that he felt it was his dad and his dad's brother Ken, who is also in spirit. The further we drove along the dunes, the more the magpies followed us. It was such a wonderful sight and an amazing day that we will not forget.

* * *

Shannon and I were about to leave the house to go to work; my car was parked at the front of the house on the street. As we walked down the front steps towards the car a magpie suddenly appeared in front of us. The magpie then followed us all the way to the car and sat at the kerb while we entered the car.

I thought to myself that Pop was trying to tell us something. I wasn't sure what it was until I drove my car around the corner past the local school, where there is an area for parents to drop off their children. Many of these parents double park and block the road, while other parents will overtake and drive on the wrong side of the road to get around these parked cars. This street is very narrow and is only just wide enough for two cars to pass each other if cars are parked correctly.

On this particular morning it was raining, it was school-zone time, meaning a speed limit of 40 km/h, and there were parents double parked because they didn't want to walk in the rain.

As I went around the corner I heard Pop say loudly in my ear: 'Slow up and be careful.' Luckily I was only travelling at 20 km/h because a woman in a big 4WD came speeding around the corner on the wrong side of the road, almost hitting me head-on. If I had been driving at the speed limit of 40 km/h, the woman would not have missed my car and we would have collided.

Thankfully Pop warned me of the impending danger. I hate to think what would have happened if a young child had been crossing the road at that exact time.

I am always very careful driving down this street, but since this time I am even more careful. If I see a magpie I always pay attention.

* * *

Shannon was looking to purchasing her first car. As we drove up to the seller's house to have a look at a particular car, a magpie landed right next to the driveway where the car was parked. Shannon said to me: 'I think Pop thinks this is a good car, Mum!' The magpie flew off and then we took the car for a test drive. When we returned to the house another magpie landed nearby. Yes, she did buy the car and, yes, I do think that Pop was giving us his approval.

We went back the following week to pick up the car. While I was speaking to the owner of the car, a magpie flew down right next to where we were standing. The magpie then walked up to the open car door and looked inside. I began to laugh when I saw what was happening. I then explained the story of my magpie visits. The owner said to me that he had never seen a magpie do this at his home before and he thought it was unusual that this one seemed so tame to walk up and stand with us and even look into his car.

Because Pop had always been very protective of the children, I am sure this was his way of showing me that everything was okay before I drove the car home.

* * *

Recently, I was driving Shannon to work when she said: 'I need to share something with you, Mum.' She then explained that Facebook has a section where your memories come up onto your page. She said: 'Mum, I want to read out to you what Ryan wrote on his memories page this morning. It says: "When I was 21 years of age, I had everything."' He had posted a picture of himself with Grandma and Pop. When Shannon told me this I burst into tears; they were tears of sadness, but most of all they were tears of pride. I thought, what a beautiful thing for my son to say, not to mention how much of an influence Grandma and Pop had on my children's lives.

* * *

Since Pop's passing he has gone to great lengths to give us signs from above.

Warwick is now a true believer of the signs that his dad constantly shares with all of us, to keep his memory alive. We, as a family, do truly believe in his signs from above and that he is only a thought away.

CHAPTER 6

Antique Tales

Tas Psarakis is a client of mine, who lives in Sydney. I had the pleasure of meeting him approximately ten years ago.

Tas has an interest in the American Civil War and some years back he went to a coin-and-banknote auction in Melbourne. Tas visited the auction in the hope that he might be able to purchase some interesting antique items to add to his collection. While at the auction, Tas perused the catalogue and came across a number of items: militaria, medals, tokens and badges. He also saw a tintype photograph of a United States Civil War soldier. Tas has always been drawn to the American West without any explanation as to why. But at this point he really hadn't collected many items from this time.

Two weeks after Tas returned from the coin-and-banknote auction, the photograph of the Civil War soldier kept popping into his head.

As the image was so strong in his mind he decided to return to the auction house to see whether the photograph had sold or not.

Tas flew back down to Melbourne and was excited to discover that the photograph of the soldier was still there. He felt an overwhelming urge to purchase the photograph and was extremely happy that he was able to procure the image for a good price.

Original Tintype photograph of McGlinchy, before restoration

On his return to Sydney he took the photograph to have it professionally restored, copied and enlarged. The original image was quite small and had suffered some slight wear and tear. After the restoration and enlargement the image of 'McGlinchy' came to life.

The image was of a Union cavalryman and had been taken in a studio with a painted background. The soldier is standing, dressed in full uniform. He is awkwardly holding a revolver across his chest with his left hand, and in his right hand he has a sword drawn and pointing skywards. He has his scabbard positioned next to his left leg.

Restored image of McGlinchy

The background is a painted image of the countryside with a large number of tents standing side-by-side in rows. There is an image of a soldier standing in front of a tent. The soldier in the painted background is in full uniform and he is standing at attention as if he is guarding the tent. There is a flag on the top of the tent. Unfortunately, I can't seem to find any clues about what the flag represents. I feel that the flag is connected to the Cavalry unit of the time.

The most interesting thing about the photograph is that the floor where McGlinchy is standing appears to be carpeted. The poor man's clothes seem to be ill-fitting and his expression is awkward, giving the impression that he doesn't want to be in the picture.

The photograph gives no indication of what the soldier's rank or regiment was and there is nothing to identify who this mysterious soldier was. However, Tas thought that the photograph was simply a wonderful piece of American military history.

* * *

Tas decided that he would book in with me for a reading. As a matter of interest, Tas thought that he would bring the photograph of the unknown American soldier. As soon as I opened the door and let Tas into my office for his reading I began smiling at him and I told him that he had a photograph with him that I needed to tune in to. Tas came into my reading room and so did the energy of the unknown American soldier. As soon as Tas gave me the photograph I held it in both hands and closed my eyes to tune in to its energy.

I immediately began to receive information about the soldier in the photograph. I could see where he served and I began to learn about his family. The man was a very gentle soul, who told me that he didn't really want to be a soldier, but at this time in history men didn't really have a choice. The man told me that he was of Irish origin and his surname was McGlinchy (or possibly spelt McGlinchey or McGlinchay). When I looked further into the name there are a number of different ways of spelling it. During the 1800s a lot of people couldn't spell, so people wrote down the name the way they thought it sounded. McGlinchy was apparently quite a common name in the 1800s in America. Researching the name is like trying to find someone by the surname of Smith – there are a large number of them.

I asked the man what his Christian name was. I was given a 'D' sound and I thought his name could have been Daniel, David or Donald. I also questioned if he was a Jnr – meaning that he may have been named after his father or grandfather. The other name that popped into my head, was James. I wasn't sure if this was another family connection, however.

On researching the name of McGlinchy, I found that there are a number of Daniels and a smaller number of Davids with this surname. There is a David Daniel McGlinchy; I couldn't find any Donalds, however there are a very large number of James McGlinchys. A James McGlinchy has a son called Daniel Francis. James McGlinchy was born in Ireland and he was a Civil War soldier.

McGlinchy told me that his family had migrated from Ireland and then moved to Newfoundland. He said that his family had moved down to an American state that was close to the American/Canadian border. I was given the impression that McGlinchy could have been born in the United States and that his parents were migrants.

McGlinchy had light brown, slightly wavy hair, and he had kind grey/blue eyes and a moustache; he was of medium build and I could see that he stood at around 5'7"–5'9" in height. He appeared to me to be a very proud man, with a quiet demeanor. He was quietly spoken and I felt that his family was everything to him. He had experienced a very challenging life and I felt that he had suffered significant losses in his family.

McGlinchy told me that he had at least two brothers and I felt that the brothers could also have been enlisted in the military. I got the feeling that he came from a large family. I also felt that he had sisters, but he didn't mention anything about them to me.

McGlinchy told me that he was married and he had four children. He had three daughters and one son. He suffered many hardships during this life and his wife died at a young age while she was in childbirth with their youngest child. His eldest daughter was around twelve years of age at the time his wife died, and she took on a mother's role, helping to raise her younger siblings.

McGlinchy spoke to me about his military career. He told me that he was in the Cavalry – first the 42nd, and then the 44th. He mentioned the city of Wyoming, but I was not sure if that was the Wyoming Cavalry unit he was a member of or not. But there is a David McGlinchey, who was in the 2nd Cavalry of Massachusetts and who deserted and then rejoined the 4th Cavalry of Massachusetts. I'm not sure if there is a connection to this man.

He showed me how he had travelled from the upper northern states of the United States close by, to the Canadian border. He told me that it was very cold and quite a miserable time for him as he was constantly out in the elements.

He showed me the images of huge herds of bison grazing on the plains and I feel that this was a significant time in his life. He showed me how hot it could get and then he showed me the change of the seasons and how he struggled with his horse in the snow while he stayed with the herd.

McGlinchy told me that he had a connection to farming and I felt that it could be something his family had done in Ireland.

He expressed to me how he hated the war and didn't like the conflict, however he was a proud man who felt he needed to do his duty for his country and wear his uniform with pride. I could see that he was a soldier in the American Civil War and he was a member of the Union.

He showed me that he had lived in a two-storey mansion in the North before joining the army. I felt that he had to give up his home once he joined the Cavalry.

McGlinchy mentioned that he could have some family who lived in Louisiana.

McGlinchy spoke to me about his life in the Cavalry and about being an escort of the wagon trains that migrated across the western plains. I was shown images of the railway being built and the wagon trains that followed the progress. I was shown wagon trains travelling along the prairies; I could see the journey that the wagon train underwent to reach the group's final destination. I was shown the symbol of a modern-looking highway marker with the number 54 on it. I wasn't sure what this meant, but I knew that the number was important because McGlinchy showed it to me a number of times. I could also see that this was possibly the route that the wagon trains could have travelled. When I saw the number I was also shown the image of railway workers building the railway lines.

Route 54 is an east-west United States highway that runs northeast-southeast for 2,115 km. It runs from Griggsville, Illinois, to El Paso, Texas. The Union Pacific Railroad's Tucumcari Line (formerly called the Southern Pacific and Rock Island Lines 'Golden State Route') runs parallel to Route 54 from El Paso to Pratt, Kansas. The train route encompasses approximately two thirds of Route 54.

McGlinchy showed me that the wagon trains were mostly occupied by women and children, due to many of the men being enlisted in the military. I could see that McGlinchy's children were travelling with him in one of the wagons during the migration. His eldest daughter was driving the wagon when the wagon train was attacked by native American Indians. I witnessed McGlinchy being ordered to shoot three of the Indians while trying to protect the wagon train. McGlinchy didn't think that it was necessary to shoot, however he followed orders. McGlinchy showed me how he had great remorse about the shootings and he told me that this had been something that had haunted him for his entire life.

Tas, his daughter Sophia, and son-in-law Victor have conducted initial research into the United States Army archives and they found that there was indeed a soldier with the surname of McGlinchy. This soldier was in the 42nd Massachusetts Cavalry and was later transferred to the 44th. Initial research showed that this regiment was probably assigned to wagon train escort that travelled from the northern states to the South.

Tas later looked up the Santa Fe cut-off trail that ran from Dodge City, Kansas, to Santa Fe, New Mexico. He has told me that further research is required. The information that came up during the reading about McGlinchy certainly fits the records.

I have since seen Tas a number of times for readings concerning other matters, as well as for the mystery soldier named McGlinchy. On one occasion I was shown that Tas was in fact McGlinchy in a past life. Bizarre as this might seem, it would also explain Tas's avid interest in the Civil War and the history of the 1800–1900s of the United States. Tas is of Greek descent, yet he has always been drawn to the United States.

McGlinchy's message to Tas was this:

I have been you and you have been me. Live in the now. You can't change your past. I am pleased that you have learnt of me. Protect your family. I will always be with you.

After I channelled this message from McGlinchy I had to wipe tears from my eyes as I could feel the raw emotion that McGlinchy had been feeling.

It is so interesting for Tas that visiting an antique fair and, by chance, purchasing a tintype photograph of an unknown soldier, has uncovered a lot of information and the introduction to a past life that Tas didn't know existed. Tas has told me that this discovery has proved to be a very enlightening experience indeed.

* * *

Tas, Sophia and Victor have visited America and visited the towns on the Route 54 highway. Tas has reported that he felt very at home in a lot of the towns and he felt that there was a familiarity and deja-vu moments along the way.

He has always been drawn to the weapons that were used during the American Civil War. Tas is an avid clay-pidgeon shooter and a gifted marksman.

I wonder if any of his memories from his past life have followed him into his current incarnation. Tas has a personality very similar to

McGlinchy's. He is very soft and gentle and he is a family man who has two wonderful daughters and a beautiful granddaughter named Isabella. His appearance is not that much different to McGlinchy's – he has blue/grey eyes, brown hair and is of medium build. He is 5'5" in height – a little shorter than McGlinchy.

CHAPTER 7

Memories Not Forgotten

My psychic abilities came to the fore after I miscarried my second child, a daughter, whom I would have named Brooke, had she survived. After this incident my psychic abilities opened up and could not be shut down. This was an extremely traumatic time in my life and at times it was terrifying to witness the daily visions that I was being shown by the spirit world.

After the miscarriage I was told that I would most likely not be able to conceive any more children, due to numerous health issues. Deep down in my heart I knew that this was not the case. I could feel that there were other little souls waiting to be born into my family.

Two years after the miscarriage occurred I fell pregnant with my beautiful son, Blake. This was a time of great joy, but also a time of great torment as my psychic abilities were growing stronger and stronger and I still found it very hard to control them.

During the pregnancy I worried what the visions and psychic experiences would do to my unborn child. To help calm me and alleviate the stress from my new psychic gifts, I did a lot of meditation and would listen to the singer Enya, to help me relax.

My boys, Ryan and Blake, were born one day and four years apart. Blake was born on 31 March 1994 and Ryan was born on 1 April 1990. My paternal grandfather, Bernard Ernest Gee, shares the same birthday as Ryan; and for a moment, there, I thought that both boys would share the same birthday. However, I think Blake was a little too impatient to wait another 24 hours before arriving into this world.

From the moment Blake arrived, he was very aware of the spirit world. He was very different to Ryan. He was a very nervous baby and was not very cuddly like his older brother. If I had the window open and the curtains in the room moved with the breeze, he would become hysterical until I closed the window and the curtains stopped moving. It was quite difficult to get him to settle. The only way I could settle him was to play music by Enya, which I am sure he heard while he was in utero.

Blake had a true mind of his own and was more interested in playing with our dog, Schooner, than playing with his brother. He was happy to go outside into the backyard and make guns out of sticks, or find other pretend weapons that he would use to play with his invisible friends.

He was always frightened of the dark and extremely frightened of heights.

From the moment he could talk he would tell me about the men who would come into his room and frighten him. On numerous occasions he would tell me that 'The Men' were back in his room. When I asked him about 'The Men' he would just stop talking and tell me that he didn't want to talk about them anymore.

One day, when he again mentioned 'The Men', I asked him what the men looked like. He said that they had their arms or legs missing. He said some of them had nails in their heads and they were bleeding. He said that they were dressed in green clothes and some of them were wearing helmets.

He would describe 'The Men' in his room on numerous occasions and it made it difficult for him to go to sleep. When the boys shared the same room the issue with 'The Men' became more confronting, as both of the boys began to experience unusual events in their bedroom. At night, to help the boys to sleep, I would read books to them and then lie in their room with them until they feel asleep.

At about four years of age Blake became very interested in the First and Second World Wars. My children have a number of family members who were in the Second World War and this is the reason that we thought he may have become so interested in the armed forces. One day when we were looking at a book about ANZAC Day, Blake said that the men in his room looked like the ones in the book. The picture was of men in their battle fatigues, in green army uniforms, and with helmets on their heads. Finally, I began to understand who my children's mysterious visitors were.

ANZAC Day became a very special occasion for our family, especially for Blake. He was always very adamant that we attend the ANZAC Dawn Service because he would tell us that we couldn't let our mates down. He said that we needed to 'Remember Them!'

From the age of about five, until he was in his early teens, he always wanted to wear army camouflage clothing. An American friend of the family gave him a whole lot of children's-size reproduction army camouflage clothing that her son had grown out of. Any clothing that was in camouflage colours or had any connection to the army became a part of his wardrobe. Another friend of ours was a member of the

Army Reserve and gave Blake some army-issue camouflage paint, which he proudly wore when he was dressed in his army clothes. If his army clothes were dirty or in the wash, he would refuse to wear anything else until they were clean and dry.

I thought his interest in the Wars was just a stage he was going through and I thought that he would grow out of it. I now realise that there was so much more to this connection.

* * *

When he was 6–7 years old Blake began to hear spirit speaking with him. He had an old man in spirit, who suddenly appeared in his life. The spirit was not a particularly nice person and my son would tell me that the man would frighten him and swear and yell at him. I used to work on the Haunted Sydney Ghost Tours during the time the old man entered Blake's life. I became worried that it was my fault – that maybe the old man, in spirit, had followed me home after a tour and befriended Blake. When I would ask Blake about this unpleasant man he would tell me that the man didn't want me to know about him. One evening when he was going to bed he told me that the man was with him and he was frightening him. This particular night was quite challenging because, as the night wore on, I too began to see the man who had been hanging around and causing Blake distress.

I lay down in bed beside Blake and comforted him in my arms. I had known for some time that my grandfather was an ancestral guardian angel of both of my boys, so I decided it was time to ask for his assistance. I called in both of my grandparents to assist with protecting Blake from the unwanted visitor. I then called for assistance from as many angels as I could muster. I visualised the bedroom filling with protective white heavenly light from above. We both could see the energy shifting in the room as the light began to appear.

I asked Blake to tell me about the man. He said the man was dirty and he had grey hair, had missing front teeth and he would use swear words when he spoke to him. He said that his clothes were all ripped and dirty and he didn't have any shoes on his feet. Blake said that the man was an old man, about the age of his Poppy. He then said that he saw the man in a building and that there was a fire. He said that was how the man had died. He went on to describe that the man was in an old building and that someone threw a glass bottle with liquid inside it. There was a piece of paper stuck into the top of the bottle and it was on fire.

I couldn't believe that my six-year-old son was describing what is known as a 'Molotov cocktail'. No wonder my poor little darling didn't want to talk to me about the man, and no wonder he was so frightened to go to sleep at night.

The spirit who had been terrorising Blake for the last few months then began to tell me his story. He told me his name was William and he had fallen on hard times and he had lived in Kings Cross. When he told me this I realised that he had in fact followed me home from one of the Ghost Tours I had worked on, as the tours left from a car park in Kings Cross.

William then went on to explain that he had died in a fire. I have since looked up fires in Kings Cross and there was a fire on Darlinghurst Road in December 1975 at the Savoy Hotel, Kings Cross. William then explained that he was an alcoholic and, because of this, he had lost contact with his family and had resorted to living in Kings Cross.

I told William that he did not belong in our house and he should not be hanging around my son and frightening him. He then told me that he wasn't trying to scare Blake – he just wanted someone to talk to. William said that he followed me home one night after I had been to Kings Cross, because he could see my 'light'. He said that not many people glowed like I do and he knew that when he saw this light it meant the person could see him and communicate with him.

William said that he had been trying to get my attention for some time, but when I didn't notice him he went to visit Blake because he had the same 'light' around him that he saw around me.

I told William that it was time to leave and I said that I was going to send him into the light so that he could reunite with his family and finally be at peace. At first William was not too impressed about my offer. He told me that he wasn't always a good person and he was worried that he wouldn't be able to go to Heaven. I explained to William that everyone who chooses to transition into the light is welcome and that there was no need to worry.

When I began to describe his family and when I told him that his wife and family were waiting to reunite with him, he began to smile. William said that he had been waiting for a very long time to see them again. His one wish was that his family would forgive him for being an alcoholic. I told him that he didn't need to worry – his family were clearly waiting for him to join them.

Blake then said to me: 'Mummy, can you see the light? It is getting really bright in here.' I could certainly see the light. I focussed on bringing it in, making it brighter and brighter. I asked William to hold my hand and told him that I would accompany him on his journey walking into the light. In my mind's eye I visualised that William and I were walking up a stairway leading into Heaven.

I asked Blake if he could see what was happening and he said he could. I walked with William, leading him to meet his family. The light then began to surround us; it was so bright and welcoming.

Once William took his wife's hand he turned to me and smiled, flashing me his toothless grin. The look on his face was priceless.

Blake then said to me: 'Mummy can you hear them?' I asked Blake what he was hearing and he said that the angels were singing. He said that they were singing 'Hallelujah, Hallelujah!' Then he said he couldn't see or hear William anymore, and he closed his eyes and went to sleep.

The whole event felt like a dream. The following morning I asked Blake if he remembered what had happened and he simply said that William had gone to Heaven. And then that was the end of the conversation.

From that point onwards I have always been extremely careful to clear myself after visiting any historical locations. I don't want to bring any unwanted visitors back home with me.

The whole incident reaffirmed my thoughts that Blake is very psychic. I knew that it would be very important for me to help him to understand his gifts when, and if, he wanted to use them in the future.

* * *

After we had the experience with William I began to pay more attention to Blake when he spoke about 'The Men' in his room. At times he would talk about war and tell me that one day he was going to join the Army and help his mates protect our country. Because he was so interested in the Army and the history of the World Wars, I planned a special surprise for him. We went to visit the Victoria Barracks in Paddington, Sydney, to watch the soldiers on parade. We also visited the Victoria Barracks War Museum, where he was fascinated with the different uniforms, weapons and, of course, the war medals.

After our visit to the Victoria Barracks, Blake became even more interested in soldiers and the war. My father-in-law, Bob ('Poppy'), would play armies with him and they would hide out in the backyard, away from enemy lines. Poppy would make a fire and boil the billy to have 'Billy Tea' and they would eat ANZAC biscuits together.

* * *

Fast forward to 2015, and Blake turned 21 years of age, which was also the 100th Anniversary of the landing at Gallipoli during the First World War. We had hoped to be picked out of the ballot to go to Gallipoli to be present at the Dawn Service. However, it wasn't to be. Instead we went to our local Dawn Service ceremony to 'Remember Them'.

We had our alarms set so we would not sleep in. The morning was very cool and crisp and there was a slight breeze in the air as we walked down to our local epitaph and waited for the ceremony to begin. The crowd was much bigger than it had been in previous years and the feeling of anticipation amongst the crowd was very strong.

I felt quite emotional this year and felt that something significant was going to take place. I wasn't sure what I was expecting to happen, but I just knew that today was a very special day. It wasn't until the service finished and we returned home that I found out what it was.

I had decided that I would begin to write more chapters for this book, when a little voice in my head told me that I should look up my grandfather's service records. As it was the 100th Anniversary of Gallipoli, all of the service records for the First World War Veterans were available online.

I put my grandfather's name, Bernard Ernest Gee, into the service records, forgetting that he was in the Second World War. Due to him being in the Second World War his records were not available to access for free. However, I could see a similar name on the screen that kept popping up in front of me. The soldier's name was Walter Ernest Gee.

At first I thought that I was doing something wrong, so I closed the tab down on the computer screen and I put my grandfather's name back into the search engine. Again, Walter Ernest Gee came up and jumped out at me. This time the soldier's name seemed to be glowing at me. I tried one more time to delete his name and re-enter my grandfather's name. On this attempt I finally realised that the records were only open for servicemen from the First World War. Once again, this same name popped back onto the screen. I always believe in the old saying 'third time lucky'. So, as this was the third time that this had happened, I became curious as to why this name kept jumping out.

I didn't think that my father's family had any relatives that came from that part of NSW, but nevertheless I thought I would have a look at this man's service records. When I did open up his files I couldn't believe my eyes. What stood out to me immediately was that Walter was born exactly 100 years before Blake, on the same date. As far as I know, this man is not related to my immediate family, however I am sure that somewhere along the line this connection is more than a coincidence.

You are probably reading this and saying to yourself, so what? This is just a coincidence. I then looked at how old Walter was when he enlisted in the army. He had been 21 years of age – the same age as Blake.

Walter was 5 feet, 11 inches tall, but another military record had his height at 5 feet, 4 inches tall. He had brown eyes and light-brown hair, although some of the other information says his hair was red. He was a labourer before joining the Army. When he enlisted in the Army he was a gunner. The more I read about him the more information I wanted to discover.

Blake has brown eyes and light-brown hair, he is 6 feet, 3 ½ inches tall, and when he was little he wanted to be a gunner in the Army. When he was in his early teens he thought about doing an apprenticeship in the building trade.

When Blake was a little boy he always spoke about the men that were left behind in the War and how important it was to remember them. I wondered if there was really a connection between my son and Walter. Could Blake be remembering a past life? I know this does sound a little strange, but could this be possible? After all of the experiences I have had, since discovering my psychic abilities, nothing ceases to amaze me.

Walter returned to Australia in 1919. He was awarded a mention* in dispatches, for his bravery while serving in the First World War.

*(One of the oldest Imperial forms of recognition for bravery or distinguished service is when a serviceman or servicewoman is 'mentioned' in dispatches.

A dispatch is an official report, written by a senior commander in the field, to pass on information about the progress of military operations. Commanders would include in their dispatches the names of those deserving attention to their services. Mentions may be for a specific act of bravery or for a period of outstanding service.

If your name appeared in these lists you were said to have been 'mentioned in dispatches'. The dispatches were usually published in The London Gazette, so a mention equated to a public commendation.

This, and the Victoria Cross, were the only forms of recognition for gallantry or distinguished service in action that could be made posthumously. See https://www.awm.gov.au/encyclopedia/mention-despatches)

The more I discovered about this man, the more interested I became. I started to delve a little deeper and looked at when he was discharged from the Army. I discovered that he was discharged on the date of my birthday, September 27. Yes, this could be another coincidence, or was this a sign that there was a connection?

I also found it interesting that of all the returned servicemen's records available on the internet, and of all the people in the world, for that matter, the records for Walter were the ones that jumped out at me. I really feel that Walter was trying to tell me something.

After doing some research on a number of the ancestry websites I have been able to compile a family tree of some of Walter's life and his ancestors. Some of what I have uncovered has been quite sad.

* * *

Walter lived with his mother in Sydney's eastern suburb of Randwick, until he joined the Army. When he married he moved to the southern suburbs of Sydney. He had two children, but I can only find information about a son. Walter's son was also a member of the military and tragically he died at age 23 in a car accident on Christmas Day.

My father's family came from Tasmania. When my father was younger he moved to NSW and lived in Kensington, which is only 2 km away from where Walter was born and had lived. What a coincidence that they would have both been living in the same area at the same time.

Via Google Maps I have been able to look at a number of the addresses that Walter lived in before his death. Unfortunately, most of the locations have now been redeveloped, so it is harder for me to tune in to his original property. I had hoped that I may have been able to take Blake to visit these addresses in order to see if it ignited any memories.

After scouring the Australia and New Zealand, Find A Grave Index, I successfully located the cemetery where Walter and his wife were interred. To be honest I couldn't believe my eyes when I found the location. They were interred at the Woronora General Cemetery and Crematorium. My office is located only five minutes away from the cemetery, on the other side of the railway line. I wondered if this was just another coincidence or if I was meant to find out more? I was so excited to make this breakthrough. In the past, when I have visited gravesites, I have been able to make a greater connection to the person in spirit. I hoped that this would be the case in this instance. The next part was to visit the cemetery and hopefully find out where the graves were.

The following day I visited the cemetery. I took my divining rods with me as they are also a very useful tool to help locate headstones. First stop was to the main office to see if I could obtain a map of where the graves were located. The lovely lady in the office asked me who I was looking for and I told her the names. She asked me if I was a relative and then I replied that I was doing research for a book I was writing and explained the story. The lady at the office thought that the whole story was quite intriguing and said that there was no coincidence. She promptly looked up the names and said that even though she had numbers for their burials, there were no headstones for either the names that I had. She said that the man's ashes I was looking for were scattered on grounds in an unmarked area and his wife was buried in an unmarked grave somewhere in the cemetery. The lady at the office said that during the time that they were interred the cemetery didn't keep records of the locations where ashes were scattered or buried. This was quite disappointing to hear. However, I wasn't going to give up that easily.

While doing my research on Ancestry.com, I managed to find Walter's wife's parents and her siblings and I also found that some of the family members were also buried at Woronora. I asked the lady at the office if she could look up the location of his wife's family members' headstones, in the hope that Walter's remains had been put in with them.

I was given a map that indicated the rough vicinity of the family's gravestones. I was strongly pulled to the back area of the Anglican section; however, this area was not included in the area I was given on the map. I did a quick walk halfway down one row of headstones and decided that I would go back up to the beginning of the section and start methodically walking up and down each row, to find the family. I also used my divining rods to assist me in finding where the headstones might be. I was instantly drawn to a section to the right-hand side of the Anglican section. I scoured up and down the rows for some time. I felt that I was in the right spot, but I couldn't find a headstone with the right name on it. The area my divining rods crossed at was an unmarked grave in between a row of headstones. I was puzzled why the rods had crossed at this grave and, ignorantly, I walked away.

I spent another hour walking up and down the rows, painstakingly looking for the headstone, but to no avail. I became very frustrated and I decided that today might not be the day to find Walter, or any of his family for that matter.

Feeling very frustrated, I decided to leave. But at that moment a little voice in my ear guided me down to the back section of the cemetery that was not included in the Anglican section. I couldn't help but laugh to myself because this was the first location I was drawn to when I had arrived.

Within a few moments I found what I was looking for. In a plot close to the end of the row, I managed to find a grave containing three of the man's relatives, all placed in the one plot.

I found a plot with all the names that were connected to his wife's family tree. I hoped I had found some of his wife's siblings and possibly a nephew. However, on later inspection of the family tree, the date of deaths did not match up with the information I had researched on the Ancestry.com site, even though all names were correct. I was a little disappointed not to have found any of the direct relatives.

On first entering the cemetery I hadn't noticed that each grave has a tiny little number etched into it. I noticed the numbers while looking at one particular grave. When I looked at the deceased register list that I was given at the office, I noticed the numbers for Walter's wife's parents.

I thought that I would give it one last try to find Walter, his wife and her parents. I also traced the numbers to the area that I first walked along, the place where the divining rods had crossed when I first began my search in the cemetery.

I felt quite annoyed at myself for not trusting the rods in the first place; they are always right when I am searching for something. The unfortunate thing was that the grave was unmarked and it was just an empty plot of grass. There was nothing whatsoever to say who was laid to rest at the spot.

Part of me was very excited to find that, indeed, Walter was a real person and I had been able to connect with him in some small way. However, another part of me was very disappointed that he and his wife didn't even have a plaque, headstone or a memorial to remind people that they were living beings who had been part of this Earth. I thought that this was very sad indeed. I pondered this, and questioned if a part of my journey and, in fact, Blake's journey, was to find out about Walter and to let people know that he had existed. I strongly feel that in some small way he was trying to get my attention so he wouldn't be forgotten.

I returned home disappointed that I couldn't find their headstones, and thought about how I could find out more about him and if there was some connection to him and Blake.

* * *

When I arrived home I asked Blake what his thoughts were about going under hypnosis to try to contact Walter. He was open to the idea and he said that he would give it a try. I contacted a hypnotherapist I trust. I have undergone hypnosis on numerous occasions for murder cases that I have worked on, and each of the sessions have been very successful.

I discussed what the possibilities were for Blake to find out if there was any connection to the soldier. The hypnotherapist thought that there was a very good chance, so we booked a date for the session.

As the hypnotherapist is interstate, it was arranged to do the session via Skype.

I personally haven't had hypnosis via Skype, so I hoped that it would be successful for Blake to make contact.

The day finally arrived and the hypnotherapist explained what would happen during the session. Blake was asked if there were any questions he might like to explore during the session. He wanted to know what, if any, connection he had to Walter. He wanted to know if the man had any messages for him and he wanted to know about his life. The hypnotherapist said that Blake would be put into a meditative state to let him explore the information that he was shown.

During the session Blake was taken to the battlefields in Europe during the First World War. He said that he could see the battle taking place around him. He was in the trenches, fighting with his battalion. He could see guns being fired and men being shot. He could see the wounded and he felt an overwhelming feeling of despair. He said he was aware of what was going on but was not able to be of assistance to the men he saw injured around him. He felt as if he were watching a movie and he was actually part of the movie but the other people in it were not aware of his presence. He could see the man (at the same time as being him) trying to comfort his fellow soldiers and speaking with them to help them to not focus on their fear and impending death. He could see that he was a very strong man who had a very calm demeanor, which people looked up to. Blake got the feeling that he was a very strategic person who thought about his every move. He was very good with his hands and people relied on him to get the job done.

Walter told Blake that he was him in another life, and they were one and the same. He was disappointed that he didn't fulfil his mission in life, due to the war and the mental damage it had done to him. He told Blake that he was a broken man after the war and it had destroyed the true man he was. He showed how broken-hearted he was after losing his son in a car accident at an early age. He said that this was something he found extremely hard to get over. He was even more devastated when his beloved wife died the year before he had. He also told of his final moments being alone in a hospital room, overwhelmed by sadness from the loss of his beautiful wife and son.

He showed that, since his passing, he was met by his family and was so excited about them all being together again in spirit. He then told Blake that he had been with him since birth and had tried to make his presence known when he was an infant. He was sorry for causing any alarm with the nightmares of the men with nails in their heads and missing limbs. These were some of the memories that had haunted him from his time on the battlefield.

The dreams that Blake had experienced from such an early age were the memories of his lifetime as Walter. Walter wanted Blake to know that he was now connected to him in this life – there was an essence of him in Blake's life. He had chosen to come into this life, via my son, so that he would remember who and what he had been in his past life.

The most important message was that Blake needed to follow his heart and to do what needs to be done. He was chosen for a reason and he should never ever give up on his dreams.

He wanted to affirm that his and Blake's birthdates were extremely important and that there was no coincidence that the two men were born on the same day, exactly 100 years apart. History did repeat for a reason and this time, together, they would achieve their goals.

Blake said that during the hypnosis session he could see numbers flying past him at great speed. He could see time moving and he could feel consciousness shifting. He felt that personality and consciousness was a mathematical equation that was created through images. He was given the image of a pyramid and the numbers 3 and 1 and he was shown a straight line that connected the two numbers. He was told that the surname GEE was equal to the number 3 and that the 1 represented a system that created it all.

* * *

When Blake came out of the hypnosis session he was extremely tired. He said that he was very aware of what he had seen and felt. He asked me where the information came from because it had felt so real. He then began to question whether it was his imagination that had connected him with Walter, or whether it was a real experience he had. Personally I have undergone hypnosis on seven occasions and the feeling is quite surreal, to say the least. I asked him to think about the information he received and to question if it felt real or not. He said that he felt that he was truly in the war and he was present on the battlefield, with the battalion, during a battle. He could see the men in the trenches and he felt like he was one of them. He could also feel what life was like when he was Walter in life, and he felt that the two of them were connected in some way. He said that Walter had told him that he would always be with him and that he was one of his guides. Blake was pleased that the hypnosis experience reminded him that he could achieve the hopes and dreams that Walter wasn't able to in his lifetime.

* * *

Since the hypnosis session, Blake has still been able to feel Walter's presence by his side. The whole experience has certainly assisted him and I now understand who the visitors were in his room when he was a little boy.

The most wonderful thing that has come out of this experience is that we can reconnect and understand the stories of the past. So many things now make sense of Blake's obsession with the Army. It has also put a lot of things into perspective, on a spiritual level.

I am sure our family will never look at ANZAC Day in the same way. No matter what happens, we will ensure that we 'Remember Them'. Part of life, moving forward, is to reach for the stars and fulfil your life's purpose and never give up on your dreams.

* * *

I feel so blessed that Walter has made our family aware of his existence. Through writing this chapter I know that he will not be forgotten.

Walter Gee Remembrance Certificate

CHAPTER 8

Angels Everywhere

In 2015, my husband Warwick and I travelled to Europe for a month. This was the first time either of us had ventured this far abroad and thank goodness I took my angels with me.

We landed in London at 9.30 a.m. after travelling for almost 24 hours. We had less than two hours to join a tour in Gloucester that would take us on a sunset tour of Stonehenge. Due to time constraints, this was the only tour we could do. We were in London for only three days. It was to be 'Up Close and Personal', with a small group of people, but on arrival it appeared that this was not the case. We found 'Up Close and Personal' meant 68 people on a bus.

This was a very exciting day for me as I was about to tick off one of the major things on my bucket list – to visit Stonehenge in Amesbury, Wiltshire, in the United Kingdom. Warwick and I had hardly slept on the flight over. Adrenalin was pumping through my veins at the excitement of it all, but I was also suffering with a bad case of the flu, from the long flight.

On the drive out to Stonehenge we stopped along the way to see the historic city of Bath. I was very excited about the historical spirits I might find there.

We had approximately one hour to wander through the streets of the town. What excited me most was that we were surrounded by angels. Everywhere I looked I could see angels; they were on the buildings, they were on the signs, and they were on the historical churches. Of course there were gargoyles, but who was paying attention to any of them? This day was the beginning of my enchantment with the angels on this trip, and, of course, the spirits of the past. Mind you, I had just spent the last twelve months channelling and writing about the beautiful winged beings for my *Angel Reading Cards*, so it was no wonder I had angels on my mind.

We entered into the historical bathhouse of Bath, which had been built by the Romans. What a wonderful site to behold, and my first introduction to the Roman architecture that I was going to encounter over the next month.

During my trip I had a travel buddy, apart from my husband; a little blue prototype of a dinosaur, called 'Dash', who was to accompany us on our trip. Dash is set to be the star of a children's animated movie that will be produced by a dear client and friend of mine named Carolien Foley.

Carolien is a very gifted animator and film producer and she has some amazing ideas for the movie she has written. I volunteered to take her little, blue-painted, 3D-printed creation along with me for a trip throughout Europe. I have to say my adult children were quite jealous that Dash came with me, instead of them.

Little did I know how much trouble Dash and I would get into along the way, especially at Stonehenge.

After our trip to Bath we visited a small Saxon village named Lacock.

Lacock has a wonderful history and is the site where many films have been filmed, including *Harry Potter* and *Pride and Prejudice*. We had our evening meal at Lacock and then were given time to walk around the town. We visited the site of Harry Potter's uncle's house, in the movies, and of course Dash had to have a photo opportunity there. We also visited the site outside of Lacock Abbey, where other Harry Potter movie scenes were filmed. Dash was very happy to have his photo taken outside the grounds.

While we were walking down the streets of Lacock, we passed a restaurant and inn called 'Sign of The Angel'. I told Warwick that this was the beginning of big things and that angels would be looking after both of us during our trip. He was more excited when he spotted a pub named 'The Carpenter's Arms', as he is a carpenter by trade.

When we arrived at Stonehenge the Information Centre was shut. I cannot begin to tell you how disappointed I was that I was not able to visit the shop. Now, I have to point out that I am not NORMALLY one of those people who needs to have the souvenir spoon, T-shirt or postcard of a location. BUT THIS WAS STONEHENGE and the shop WAS NOT OPEN. I had been awake for over 30 hours by this stage and I could not buy a souvenir. (Thank goodness for the internet, where I did buy a couple of souvenirs when I returned home. Sad but true!)

The large bus group we were with was going to be split into two while we entered the inner circle of Stonehenge, and we had to decide which group to go into – the first group or the second group. I was far too tired to make any decisions and my psychic abilities weren't at their peak due to my tiredness and flu. Unfortunately, we decided to go into the second group. As it was the beginning of the Summer Solstice, I also thought I could get a photograph of the sunset if I was in the second group. But the sun was still well and truly high in the sky when it was our turn to enter the sacred stones, so a sunset photograph was out of the question.

While we were waiting for our turn to walk amongst the stones, there was a shower of rain. The first group were very privileged to have a rainbow appear amongst the stones while they were in the inner circle.

When it was our group's turn to get up close and personal I was SOOOOOO excited. I had dreamed of this day ever since I was a little girl. I was now standing on this beautiful sacred site. I was living the dream, and I was up close and personal.

As psychometry is my gift, I thought that this was it; I thought I would feel something. I hoped that I would connect with energies from the past. But alas, I felt nothing. All I could feel was annoyance that there were numerous people running around me like lunatics, with cameras and selfie sticks. I thought if I stood still that I would feel something, but I still felt nothing. Nothing at all! I was so disappointed that I had travelled all the way from Australia, not slept for over 30 hours, and was unable to psychically connect. Maybe I was just too tired.

My bucket-list dream began disappearing before my eyes, so I thought I would just take some photographs – perhaps one of my husband in a panoramic shot, on my iPhone. However, I accidentally captured

Dash, my travel buddy, at Stonehenge

a picture of one of the 34 people in our group on the other side of one of the stones to him. And it just kept getting better and better.

I took Dash out of my pocket and sat him on top of one of the sacred stones. What a mistake this was! Suddenly a security guard came over to me and he began to yell at me for desecrating the stones. He asked me how dare I touch the stones and put the 15 cm dinosaur model on them, to take a photograph. He told me that I had ruined the stones forever. I had noticed prior to my awful mistake that most of the other 33 people in my group had been stepping over, touching and leaning on the stones. However, he hadn't seemed to notice this. Instead, he began to yell at me and follow me around the site like a crazy man. He then said I stepped on a stone and ruined it, which I didn't. I did get a great photograph of Dash sitting on one of the stones, though, so I guess the embarrassment was worth it.

However, the sun did not go down while we were on the sunset tour; it probably went down an hour or so after we left. I cannot begin to tell you how sad I felt that I did not get my sunset shot of the stones, after having travelled so many miles for this very special day.

For the mishaps I was supposedly causing to the sacred site, I am sorry. The most embarrassing thing was that the other 33 people in the group were now staring at me like I was some sort of monster. They had all heard the security guard yell at me. I hoped that they would all forget about what he had said; I had to spend the next 1 hour and 49 minutes with them back to Gloucester before we were dropped off.

Day one of my dream holiday had not quite gone to plan. All I wanted to do was get back to the hotel and go to bed. The ultimate disappointment was when I got back to the hotel and looked at my photographs. Out of the 100 photographs I had taken, only three images of the inner circle were without other people in them. Oh, well. Such is life.

The one thing I couldn't believe was the fact that Stonehenge was much smaller than I had ever imagined. I expected the stones to be huge and the site to be much bigger. It certainly was surprising at how compact the site was.

Our next stop in England was on the Big Bus, to explore London. During our travels on the Big Bus we heard about the antique markets at Notting Hill, on Portobello Road. We were lucky enough to be in London on the day that the markets were open, so we decided to go and have a look.

We walked up to Notting Hill and tried to find where the markets were. We didn't realise that things don't open as early in England as they do in Australia, so we decided to go and have a cup of tea.

As we sat in the cafe we looked out of the window and could see quite large numbers of people coming up from the Underground and then disappearing down a small street. When we finished our tea we decided to follow the crowd to see if we could find the markets.

Everyone was turning off into a very narrow laneway, so we did the same. We couldn't believe our eyes when we entered the laneway. There were hundreds of people ahead of us walking past a multitude of stalls. As I love shopping I was pretty excited by all of the stalls along the footpath.

As we walked further down the street we came to a lot of shops that had small shopfronts that opened up to three separate floors of antique sellers. I was in Heaven. I could feel the energy of all of the antique pieces pulling me in all different directions. I couldn't believe how powerful the energies of the past were, here. What I loved most was all the antique and vintage jewellery.

It was an unusual feeling for me to be drawn to antiques; I am always very cautious because I have had a few disasters in the past with buying second-hand items. Visiting this location had a completely different feeling. At one shop I was drawn to a case with a fairy in it and some antique medals with angels on them.

I was mesmerised by the angel medals and really felt that they were talking to me. I walked away from them, but the medals kept calling me back. Part of my brain was thinking, what are you doing buying second-hand antique items? and the other part was saying how much I needed to buy them.

The angel medal I purchased on Portobello Road in London.
This is the angel that protected me during my trip

I am happy to say that I did purchase the two sterling silver angel medals and the sterling silver fairy. All of these items were dated from 1890–1905.

These medals became my protective mascots for our time in Europe, and they certainly worked pretty hard for the rest of our trip.

* * *

The following day it was time to leave London and travel by train to Paris. We woke up to a freezing rainy day. We caught a cab from the front of our hotel in Kensington. The cab was a typical black London cab, but a newer model than you usually see in London. Our cab driver was really lovely and he was happy to chat to us about our time in London and about where we were going to next. Warwick was the self-appointed guardian of our travel documents and passports, so when it was time to get out of the cab I quickly grabbed my bags and alighted. The interior of the cab was black and the travel documents were in a black zip-up wallet. For a split second before getting out of the cab, I thought I saw them on the back seat. As we both of separate doors on either side of the cab, and I had left the cab first, I just assumed that Warwick had picked up the wallet. We paid the cab driver and he gave us a wave and drove off into the bleak rainy London morning.

We had two hours before we needed to catch the Eurostar to Paris. I asked Warwick if he had our tickets and passports and he said he thought they were in the bag. I told him that I thought I saw them on the back seat of the cab before I got out and asked him if he had picked them up. He hadn't!

I began to panic; I could feel the colour draining from my face when I realised that we didn't have any of our travel documents, tickets, passports and, worst of all, the duplicate copies of our licences, passports and credit cards. The two vintage, sterling silver angel medals and the silver fairy were also inside the wallet, for safe-keeping. We had absolutely no ID on us and here we were in London about to go to Paris.

My mind started racing and I thought maybe I was mistaken and the wallet was really in one of our bags. I began frantically going through every bag, checking to see, if by some miracle, the wallet had been put inside one of our suitcases or in our hand luggage. While I was looking through everything the rain started to pelt down on us, which only made the situation worse. It was freezing cold and we were both wet and getting more upset by the minute.

I looked around and could see another London cab parked a short distance away from us. I ran over to it and asked the driver if he could assist us. He asked me what colour cab we had ridden in. This has to be the funniest question anyone could ask in London, especially from another cab driver, because all of the cabs are black. He then asked if I got the number plate. Of course I didn't! This is not something you do every time you catch a cab. Maybe for future reference I should make a habit of this, though. The driver then said: 'I am sorry, lady. I can't help you!' A police van drove up next to where we were standing and I noticed there was a police dog-handler in the van. Because I have worked with the police dog squad in Australia, I thought that this might be a positive sign. I went over to the officer and explained the situation and asked if he could assist us.

The officer also asked if I had got the number plate of the cab, or the driver's ID. When I told him I hadn't, he suggested that I call the hotel we were staying at in case the cab driver had returned the documents there. I called the hotel and the person who answered the phone couldn't speak fluent English. I tried to explain that we had left our travel documents in the cab and that I was trying to see if the cab driver had returned them to the hotel.

Finally, the voice at the other end of the phone understood what I was asking of him. When he said he was sorry, and that he couldn't help us, I became so frustrated and upset about our situation that I began to cry.

I turned to our bags and had one more fruitless look in them, just in case I had missed something. I suddenly felt an overwhelming calmness come over me and I could hear my guardian angel telling me not to worry – everything was going to be fine. The gentle loving voice in my right ear explained that all I needed to do was to be patient and visualise the driver of the cab coming back with our documents. As I heard these words a beautiful white feather floated down from above and gently landed at my feet.

I listened to the gentle calming voice of my angel and I slowly closed my eyes and concentrated on creating the vision of the driver coming back with the wallet. I stood there for about fifteen minutes, focussing on his return. Suddenly, the voice appeared in my right ear again and said: 'Don't worry, everything is okay!' Then he told me to turn around and face the direction in which the cab had driven off. As I did so the cab came around the corner and drove up to the kerb where we were both standing. The driver had his arm out of the window and he was holding our travel wallet in his hand. He said that he was on his way to another job when he looked back in the rear-vision mirror and saw the wallet slide across the back seat of the cab. I cannot tell you how surprised, relieved and thankful I was that this wonderful man (our Earth Angel) was so honest and thoughtful to give us back the wallet. We offered the man a tip and he refused, saying that he was happy to have been of assistance.

I told Warwick that my angel told me that the driver would come back with the wallet. He just smiled at me. He knows my connection to the angels, but I am not sure that he believes like I do. However, if it makes me happy, he is happy to accept it.

* * *

Next it was off to Paris on the Eurostar. I was so thankful to get on the train and relax after the scare of losing all of our travel documents. I was now the self-appointed guardian of them. I made sure that this time we separated the copies of the passports, cards, etc. in case (fingers crossed) anything like this happened again during our trip.

The trip to Paris took 3 1/2 hours, by train. When we arrived it was cold and rainy, like London. We checked into our hotel, then it was time to do some sightseeing.

We only had three days in Paris, so there was a lot to see in such a small space of time. Before leaving Australia we had decided to get a Big Bus ticket for each city we visited as this would show us the highlights of each city. What is great about the Big Bus is that you have the opportunity to get on and off at all of the attractions each city has to offer. We joined the Bus and were taken in and around Paris. The architecture in Paris is just incredible. I fell in love with this beautiful city. Yet again, nearly every building had images of angels moulded into it. There were statues of winged beings everywhere the eye could see. I was in Heaven.

We booked a tour of the Louvre and I was mesmerised by the detailed artworks, not only on the canvases but those on the ceilings of many of the gallery rooms. The energy of this magnificent building was incredible; I absolutely loved every moment of being there and, of course, the multitude of angelic beings constantly represented in much of the artwork.

My travel buddy, Dash, was with me every step of the way; he enjoyed getting his photo taken with the statue of 'Nike' the headless Winged Victor of Samothrace, and the Mona Lisa.

The following day we visited the Eiffel Tower. Somewhere during our visit to the Tower I picked up a stomach virus and became extremely ill. On the third day in Paris, instead of visiting more of the sights, I spent the day in bed. I was so ill a doctor had to be called as I was too unwell to even leave the room.

I was quite concerned that we might not be able to make our flight to Barcelona the following morning. Thankfully the doctor performed a miracle by giving me an injection and a prescription for the virus. I felt quite weak when I awoke, however I was able to fly and that was all that mattered.

We spent the next three days in Barcelona before joining our cruise ship. I was extremely careful about anything I ate or drank, still feeling unwell from the virus.

We took the Big Bus around Barcelona and visited Barcelona's many sights. We stayed close to the Placa Reial, which is filled with little alleyways darting off in every direction, and wonderful shops and restaurants. Above many of the alleyways were carvings of smiling angels looking down on the passers-by. The energy of Barcelona was so vibrant and uplifting.

During our stay in Barcelona I felt very safe, even though we were warned about the pick-pockets and the beggars. But on our final day in Barcelona the feeling of safety was about to change.

I suffer from Psoriasis, and prior to departing our hotel I had forgotten to buy some more Dove-brand soap. After boarding our cruise ship, I decided to go back into town to try and find a chemist to purchase some soap before the cruise departed. I left my passport back on the ship with Warwick as I thought the longest I would be away for would be two hours. I caught a cab outside the cruise terminal. The cab driver said he didn't speak much English and when he asked me where I wanted to go I asked to go to a 'pharmacia'. The driver indicated that he understood where I wanted to go, so we set off. In Paris and Spain all of the pharmacies have a big green lit-up cross at the front of the shop, which makes them easy to recognise.

I initially felt completely safe, but then suddenly I could feel my angel's presence in the cab beside me. When I am in imminent danger my guardian angels will usually touch me on the side of the face and whisper in my ear to white light myself and to be aware that something isn't right. As soon as I felt my angel's presence with me I was on high alert. I could see that the cab driver was taking me further and further away from the port and we were travelling into an area that was quite run down. He drove past one pharmacy, and then another, and then another. I began to panic and I felt that my angel was correct.

I saw another pharmacy coming up ahead and I asked him to stop there. As we approached the pharmacy he made a phone call to someone and began speaking very quickly to the other person, in Arabic. He slowed the car and pulled up in front of the pharmacy. I quickly got out to purchase the soap. He asked me if I wanted a return fare to the ship, I stupidly said 'Yes', so he waited until I returned. After all of the stress I wasn't even able to find the soap I wanted. I purchased a similar type of soap and returned to the car.

The cab driver then asked me if there was anywhere else I needed to go and I said I wanted to go to an ATM because I only had 30 Euros on me. I then quickly changed my mind when I saw his eyes light up. So I told him that I had decided I didn't need to visit an ATM and I just wanted to go back to the ship.

The cab driver was again speaking on the phone. He appeared quite animated with his conversation, laughing and getting more excited as the conversation went on. I thought that the cab driver was going to turn around and return to the ship when he suddenly drove down a deserted-looking street and then turned right into a very narrow alleyway. The alley was very long and almost too narrow for the cab to drive down.

As we drove further along, a group of eight men came out of some doorways on either side of the alleyway. The men stood in front of the cab and surrounded us, blocking our path. The cab driver was still talking to someone on the phone.

I felt sick to the stomach and I could feel my anxiety building. I yelled out to the driver, saying: 'What the hell do you think you are doing?' The driver replied in perfect English that he was taking a shortcut. I surveyed the situation and assessed whether I should take my chances staying in the cab with the driver, or whether I should make a run for it down the alleyway. I decided I was safer inside the car with one man, than taking my chances with the eight men outside the car. I quickly closed my eyes and called in as many angels as I could muster. I didn't know if they could hear me, but that was not going to stop me from calling on their protection.

Suddenly, I heard a familiar soothing voice in my right ear telling me that everything would be okay. I could feel my guardian angel's warm calming presence sitting by my side in the cab.

The men abruptly stepped aside and allowed the cab to pass. The driver hung up his phone and turned around to me with a big smile on his face. He began to tell me that he had decided to take a shortcut down the alleyway as there were markets up ahead and the road was blocked off. I sternly told the driver that I wanted to return to the ship immediately. He seemed to sense my anger and annoyance and he proceeded to head in the direction of the port.

The return trip to the port couldn't happen quickly enough. It was only when I began to see familiar landmarks that I felt at ease. I could still feel the presence of my guardian angel sitting beside me in the back of the cab. It was very comforting to know that I wasn't alone.

When we turned onto the bridge leading to the port at Barcelona, I breathed a sigh of relief. The cab driver pulled up at the cab rank, turned around and smiled at me and told me that the fare was 25 Euros, knowing that I only had 30 Euros on me. He took the money from me and refused to give me the change. I thought I was lucky to be back safe and didn't argue with him. Five Euros was a small price to pay to be safe and sound.

I returned to the ship and thanked my lucky stars and, of course, my angels, that I was given the opportunity to continue my holiday.

Later that day we sailed out of Barcelona on our cruise around the Mediterranean. Over the next fourteen days we visited Marseille, Genoa,

Florence/Pisa, Malta, Sicily, Rome, Naples, Crete, Rhodes, Kusadasi and Santorini, finishing our cruise in Athens.

Our holiday was full to the brim. I had booked tours off the ship every day we were in port. In hindsight this was maybe not the best idea if you want to have a peaceful, relaxing holiday. But it was still amazing and I would recommend you take an extra week to recover when you get home as you will be physically exhausted.

Each port we visited was incredible – the culture and history amazing. I felt very connected to Europe and I felt as though I had been there before, in a past life. On our trip to Rome and the Vatican City I had a very profound experience with Michelangelo.

The day we visited the Vatican City, Pope Francis had a meeting with some Scouts from all around the world, in St Peter's Square. The Vatican City was filled with thousands of people from all walks of life. We went on a tour through the Vatican and then to the Sistine Chapel; the beautiful angel artworks are not to be missed. The Vatican was extremely busy the day we visited, and the crowd was huge. We were herded around like a bunch of sheep, from one area to another. The most disappointing part was that you really didn't have the time to have a close look at the sights.

After waiting for over an hour we finally entered the Sistine Chapel. What I liked most was that there is no speaking in the Chapel, however some people didn't seem to understand the concept of silence. The energy in there is incredible. The moment I walked into the room I could feel something special was about to happen. While in the Chapel, photography is banned. There are security officers at every turn to enforce this rule. On the day we visited there were temporary barriers that split the Chapel into three. After passing the first barrier, we were given five minutes to stand in the middle of the Chapel to view Michelangelo's artwork. The room was filled with hundreds of people. Standing in the chapel was like being in a mosh pit at a rock concert. I stood quietly in the centre of the chapel and closed my eyes to tune in to the energy. Much to my surprise I began to receive messages from above. The words flooded into my mind in the form of mental telepathy. I felt that the person sharing the information with me was male. He was very informed about the different scenes depicted on the ceiling of the Chapel. When I asked the gentleman who he was, he seemed quite surprised by my question. He said: 'It is I, the master who painted the scenes before you. Michelangelo!'

I began to laugh. Was I hearing correctly or was it my imagination? I asked the male presence if this was true. He seemed a little annoyed that I hadn't listened to him in the first instance. What I found interesting is that I don't speak Italian, yet I could clearly understand everything that he was saying to me.

He then told me to pay attention as he pointed out the important parts of the scenes above me. He began to tell me how he couldn't believe that so many people came to see his work when in fact he hated what he had created. He was a sculptor, not a painter. He was disgusted that he was made to spend many years of his life creating the artwork, when in fact he had unfinished sculptures that needed his attention. He told me how angry he was with Pope Julius II for forcing him to undertake such a gigantic task. He pointed to areas on the ceiling where he made fun of the Pope. He showed me that in one of his pictures he painted the Pope with ears like a pig, and in another picture he had an image of two angels standing behind Pope Julius II and one of them was painted sticking his thumb up at the Pope in insult to him.

Michelangelo said that there were many hidden messages painted within each scene and that most people who looked at the images had no idea about the significance. Michelangelo had a very cheeky sense of humour that people of his time did not understand or respect. He said that people looked at his work with such admiration, yet at the time of him undertaking the work, he looked at it with loathing. What he found most amusing was that he has been remembered and revered by the Church, as one of the masters. Yet when he was alive he had been constantly ridiculed and insulted for his magnificent skills.

I found the conversation with Michelangelo to be quite fascinating. I could really feel and hear his energy. Just as I felt this incredible connection to Michelangelo become even stronger, a security guard came up to where I was standing and we were told to move on and leave the Chapel to make way for more waiting tourists.

The connection was instantly broken and I was disappointed that I didn't have more time with this amazing master from the past. I felt blessed to have been given this small insight, however. I wished that there had been more time to learn and understand more about Michelangelo and his hidden messages.

I reluctantly left the chapel and was herded into St Peter's Basilica. The Basilica is certainly a sacred place also worth visiting. In every direction I looked there were angelic beings on the walls, floors and ceiling. Angelic beauty was everywhere; there were angels in adult form, as well as little cherubs, adorning the entire space. The artworks on the Basilica's dome were incredible. We entered the Basilica in the afternoon just as the sun was starting to shine down through the dome, lighting up the Basilica with crepuscular rays. It looked as if Heaven were showering the area with protective white light. It is a memory I will hold in my mind's eye forever.

After spending some time in the Basilica, it was time to leave and re-join our tour group and head back to the ship. Visiting the Vatican City is something I will never forget, not to mention the meeting I had with the one-and-only Michelangelo.

I feel blessed to have had such an angelic, uplifting experience. I felt as if I were floating on air when I returned to the ship. Luckily for me I had this large dose of angelic energy and light. What I was about to experience the following day was going to test all of my faith in myself and my angels. There is a saying that 'Bad or good things always happen in threes!' I was about to discover that I had one more bad experience to go through yet.

* * *

Our next port of call was Naples. We were going to visit the Isle of Capri, Sorrento, and then visit the ancient city of Pompeii. On the morning of our tour we were up bright and early. We joined our tour and met our guide at the waterfront – the first part of our trip was to catch a ferry to the Isle of Capri. Our guide was a short man named Vinnie. He made constant rude jokes about women and I found him to be quite offensive.

There were large numbers of people waiting to get onto the ferry and we were, once again, herded along like sheep, into the hull of the ferry, and then herded upstairs to the seating area. The ferry transported both cars and people. The trip to the Isle of Capri took about an hour and a half and the sea was rough. Many of the people on the ferry were seasick as the ferry rolled up and down with the waves.

We finally arrived in Capri and were once again herded off the ferry. We caught the funicular from Marina Grande to the top of the island. The queues were huge so it took us about an hour to get up to the top. But believe me the view and the wait was so worth it. We were given an hour of free time to walk around at the top. We walked along some of the pathways to the lookouts and were spoilt with the gorgeous views.

The Isle of Capri is known for its perfume, so if you want to buy something a little bit different I recommend you visit one of the perfumeries. On our way back to the funicular I was drawn to the window of a little jewellery store. In the window I noticed some beautiful angel jewellery. I went inside and found some little pieces that I couldn't resist. I purchased a pair of sterling silver earrings in the shape of angels, and a matching sterling silver bracelet. Inscribed on the jewellery, in Italian, was a prayer to the angels. I also purchased a cameo pendant of a cherub made from coral.

The verse on the bracelet and earrings is this: Angelo di Dio che sei il mio custode. Illumina, custodisci, reggi e governa me, che ti fui affidato dalla Piet'a Celeste. Amen.

The most common English translation is: *Angel of God, you are my guardian, to light and guard, to rule and guide me, that I was cast upon you at the mercy of Heaven. Amen.*

I was very excited by my purchases and I felt that I had a very special connection to them. I was so happy to be taking such special mementos back with me to Australia. I actually think my new additions to my growing angel collection of mementos was much more of a blessing in disguise than I could have ever imagined.

We returned back down via the funicular to join our tour group at the allotted time in the Marina Grande. We then caught another ferry with our tour group to the city of Sorrento. The ferry ride was about an hour and the scenery was spectacular. On arrival, we boarded a bus and were taken up the winding road to Sorrento. On disembarking the bus we were given a tour of the back streets and alleyways of Sorrento.

The city was incredible. I was mesmerised by all of the different shops while meandering throughout the many alleyways that lead to the main part of Sorrento. The items on display were so different to what we see in Australia. I so wished we had more time to stop and browse this area.

We finally made it to the town square and were taken into an inlaid-wood furniture shop. This shop had the most beautiful inlaid furniture I have ever seen. We were given a demonstration of how the inlays were made and then we were given one hour to peruse the local shops. I did have a little look around the shops and found a beautiful jewellery shop that sold unusual cameos. My daughter, Shannon, also has a love of angels and fairies and I found a shop that had just the cameo I wanted to buy for her. It was small, with a blue background with a delicate lady and a tiny angel dancing upon a flower. I purchased it for her.

During our time on the cruise my husband and I had befriended four beautiful Greek/Australian grandmothers from Sydney, who were on our cruise. Mareka, Helena, Irene and Maria were all widows, who had joined the cruise for Mareka's 70th birthday. During our trip to Florence, the gorgeous Mareka had become lost and we had helped her find her way back to our tour. Since that time we had randomly met up with the lovely ladies when we partook in some of the tours. On this particular tour the four grandmothers were present.

In the square there is a four-way pedestrian crossing, which is quite confusing. As our tour group prepared to leave, Irene and Maria crossed the road with Warwick, and Mareka and Helena crossed the road with me. Unfortunately, poor Mareka fell heavily on the pedestrian crossing and injured her knee, grazing her arm, side, and leg, on the road.

The tour guide and tour group crossed the road unaware that Mareka was lying injured in the middle of the road. I assisted Mareka to her feet and asked her and Helena to wait while I ran ahead to alert our tour guide and ask him to wait for the ladies before proceeding with the tour.

Each tour group guide holds a paddle above their head, with the number of the tour group on it, so that the tour group can follow them. As our tour guide was very short it was extremely hard to see his paddle. There were also four other tour groups there at this time and Sorrento is full of alleyways. I followed what I thought was our tour group, into an alley.

As the group stopped to look at a landmark, I pushed to the front of the group only to realise it was not our tour guide. I asked if he could assist me in getting back to the square as I was lost. The guide indicated that he didn't speak English and said that he could not help me.

I began to panic. I was worried about the grandmothers I had left behind, knowing that one of them was injured, and now I didn't know where Warwick was. I at least had ID on me, but I knew Warwick didn't. I had all of our money, too. I was the only one with a mobile, so I hoped that this could be my saving grace. I could now only presume that Warwick had stayed with our tour group. The cruise liner we were travelling on was called Princess Cruises and I did have my cruise card on me. (When you do a cruise your cruise card is your ID, on and off the ship.) I decided that I should try and ring the cruise company to tell them what happened. But the cruise card number didn't work. So of course this was of no help at all.

I tried to calm myself down and retrace my steps to find my way back to the square. Initially I found the drop-off point, where we had gotten off the bus. I hoped that this was where the tour group was headed. There wasn't any bus to be seen and there wasn't anyone in the vicinity who spoke English. The few people I asked just told me that they couldn't help me.

Initially I felt very calm but as time ticked on I began to panic. I found my way up through the alleyways where we had travelled with the tour. I finally found my way back to the inlaid-wood store, but by this time Mareka and Helena were no longer there. I tried to tell the store owner that I was lost and finally someone who spoke English came to the rescue.

A gorgeous man from the store said that he would ring our tour guide and reunite me with the tour. He took me out into the square and then we tried to find the tour group. We discovered that the tour bus had departed for Pompeii. After a few frantic phone calls the man from the shop asked me to return to the shop with him and he told me that I would be joining another tour from the ship and continuing onto Pompeii with them. This man was truly an angel. I couldn't thank him enough.

A few moments later a bus stopped out the front of the store and I was called over to the bus to join their tour group. The gorgeous guide was named Francesca and she told me that she would ensure that I re-joined my tour. I told her how worried I was that I had lost the grandmothers. I was very concerned that Mareka should be looked after. The last time I had seen her she had blood running down her arm and leg and she had grazed her side and she had a very large bruise beginning to form on her ribs and her knee.

You can't imagine how shocked I was as the bus turned a corner and I suddenly saw Warwick standing on the side of the road, by himself. I quickly told the guide and I asked her to stop the bus. Thank goodness I spotted him! I hate to think what would or could have happened to him if I hadn't been looking out of the bus window! My angels must have been helping me there!

Warwick told me that the tour guide had put him off the bus and told him that he had to stay behind and find me in the square. Even though he had told the tour guide that he had no money, ID, passport or cruise card (because I had everything in my bag). This didn't seem to worry our tour guide and he said that Warwick could find his own way to Pompeii or find his way back to the ship when he found me.

I was horrified to hear what had happened. One of the reasons we booked the tours through our particular cruise was to ensure our safety. Our tour guide didn't seem to be aware of the cruise rules and, from his behaviour, he really didn't appear to care. When you book a tour with Princess Cruises they 'guarantee' that nobody will ever be left behind on their tours and the ship will never leave the port without you. Well, I have to say that this cruise ship and our tour guide had a lot to answer for as this was proving to not be the case.

On hearing this, Francesca rang our tour guide and had a heated conversation with him about what had taken place. We were told

that we could re-join our original tour group when got to Pompeii
or we could stay on Francesca's tour. To be honest I wished that I had
stayed with Francesca's group, however I wanted to see if the Greek
grandmothers had been found and I wanted to see that they were okay.

On our journey to Pompeii, I decided to wear my 'prayer for the angels'
bracelet and earrings, for some added protection. I felt that after the luck
that I had been having, I needed all of the angelic help that I could get.
I hoped that this was the last thing to go wrong, as it had now been three
bad things that had happened. Thankfully, however, we were both in one
piece and my angels had been there to assist us in our time of need.

* * *

When we arrived at Pompeii, Mareka and Helena were there. Mareka
had not received any medical attention. After I had some heated words
with our tour guide, he then told me that it was my fault for wandering
off. I told him that Mareka had been injured and I was trying to get him
to stop so that she could have medical attention.

I asked him why he hadn't helped Mareka, and he said that he didn't think
that there was anything wrong with her. Mareka showed him her injuries
and he reluctantly got her some ice and gave her a couple of bandaids. I was
extremely upset about what had happened to us and Mareka. The most
important thing, however, was that we had been reunited. I didn't want our
visit to Pompeii to be spoilt, so I tried not to think about it anymore.

I found the energy at Pompeii very interesting. In the amphitheatre,
where the gladiators trained, the energy was strong and masculine. I felt
that this area had been a sacred place for men and that women had not
been welcome in this area.

While standing near the training ground I was given glimpses of the
past. I saw flashes of men dressed as gladiators sparring with each other

with huge swords and shields. I felt privileged that I was shown these glimpses of the past and I could actually feel and see what it was like to be alive so many years ago.

In some areas I found it very hard to breathe. I began to cough uncontrollably and felt as if I were suffocating. I could smell sulphur and I could feel it burning my eyes, nose and the back of my throat. I asked Warwick if he could smell anything and he said that he couldn't. I knew that I was tuning in to the psychometry of the area and picking up the tragedy of the past.

Our guide then told us that the area we were moving through was where many of the occupants had been found mummified in the streets, having died from the fumes of the volcano. They had then been covered with lava until the area had been excavated. This confirmed my sensations. The further along the street we walked, the heavier the feeling became. I could also feel the sadness and despair of the souls of the past. I felt this location had been frequented by families, and I was given glimpses of women and children running for their lives. If I had more time at the location I am sure that I would have been able to tune in to their stories further. One day I want to return to Pompeii to spend more time there. It would be wonderful to be able to open up a vortex and send the trapped souls at the location into the light, to make their journey to the other side.

* * *

On our arrival back at the ship we took Mareka to the ship's doctor to check her injuries. She was given an x-ray on her knee and her ribs. Thankfully she didn't have any broken bones; she did however have a lot of bruising and grazing on her arm, leg and ribs.

While we were waiting for the doctor, I told Mareka about how I had called in the angels to make sure that we would all be okay. I showed Mareka my 'Prayer for the Angels' bracelet and earrings that I had purchased on the Isle of Capri. I told her about my work with angels and how I felt that they had assisted us during the day. Mareka just smiled and gave me a big hug and told me that I was her angel for looking after her.

I was so pleased that everything had worked out in the end. I had a chat to my angels and said that, as I had now had three challenges, I hoped that now three good things would happen.

I think my angels were really listening to me, as I had lots of wonderful experiences on the rest of our trip. The Greek Isles were incredible and I fell in love with Santorini and Athens. I hope that one day I will return to the beautiful Mediterranean shores for a longer visit. The one thing I am certain of is that I will be taking my angels with me just in case I need a hand.

* * *

Dash also made it back to Australia in one piece. He had lost an arm in England, but after a little bit of super glue, he was almost back to new. He did lose some colour along the way and he had a lot of amazing photographs to show of his adventures.

CHAPTER 9

Angels At Uluru

In 2015, I had made plans to create another card deck when I finished writing this book. One of the locations I chose for my inspiration and astro-photography project was Uluru. I booked accommodation at Voyages Resort during August 2016, whilst they were hosting an Astronomy weekend. I have wanted to visit Uluru since I was a little girl. It has been one of the things on my spiritual bucket list.

During the time of my planned visit there was an art installation called the 'Field of Light' by Bruce Munro. The installation is made up of over 50,000 frosted-glass spheres on stems powered by solar energy. As the sun sets the 'Field of Light' comes to life in a myriad of colours.

The plan was to attend the Astronomy weekend and then take a helicopter flight over Kata Tjuta and Uluru, to take photographs. We were then going to join a special dinner experience called 'Sounds of

Silence' and then walk through the 'Field of Light' to photograph the display, including Uluru and the night sky.

My husband, Warwick, and I flew to Uluru to begin our journey. The flight over Uluru prior to landing at the airport was amazing. I was in awe of how beautiful the 'Rock' truly is. Once we landed, we headed to the resort and took it easy for the rest of the day. On the Thursday we booked to go on a bus transfer to Uluru to do a self-guided tour of the base of the 'Rock'.

Words cannot describe the emotion I felt when I arrived at the drop-off point. Uluru is such a powerful creation of nature, and here I was now standing in front of it. I couldn't wait to begin our walk. I was so excited to begin capturing images of this majestic location.

There are a number of tracks that meander around the bottom of the Rock. We decided to do the Mala walk to Kantju Gorge. As we wandered over to a small cave named Kulpi Nyiinkaku, I could hear voices. I couldn't understand what they were saying, but it was as if I was listening in to a conversation. I felt very drawn to this location and I could feel all of the hairs on my right arm stand on end. When I get this type of reaction to a location I know that I am in the presence of some very strong spirit energies.

Kulpi Nyiinkaku is where the young Nyiinka (bush boys) would camp in the kulpi (cave). The Nyiinka were taught by their grandfathers to hunt in traditional ways, at this location. This experience was a form of education where the young boys would become men.

I began to take photos of the cave while standing near the information sign. At first my camera picked up some lens flair then suddenly the energy of the location changed and a strong breeze began to surround me. As I took more photos in sequence, a beautiful circular ray of rainbow light entered the frame on the left-hand side of my camera. The energy of this light moved up and down and, at times within the pictures, images of Aboriginal art appeared within the light.

I have never experienced anything so special before in my life. I truly didn't want to leave the location. I was happy just to stay there with the beautiful energy I was seeing and feeling. Warwick began to get pretty frustrated with me, though, as he called out for me to catch up to him and visit the other cave named Kulpi Mutitjulu. This cave was full of Aboriginal cave paintings. The pictures were beautiful. Some of the images that were painted on the cave walls were similar to what my camera had picked up with the spirit energy photographs. It was interesting that I didn't get the same feeling at this location, though. The cave was beautiful, but it didn't have the same energy.

We then walked around to the Mutitjulu waterhole. This was also another wonderful energy location. There had been rain in the days prior to our visit so the waterhole was quite full.

We did the return walk to the drop-off point and then decided to walk to the southern side of Uluru along the Mutitjulu walk. Along this track there is also a very special waterhole that is the home of Wanampi, an ancestral water snake, which is part of the Aboriginal Dreamtime and a very important area for the Anangu people.

There was also water in that waterhole, but the energy here was quite different to what I had felt at the Mutitjulu waterhole. In this area the breeze was quite still, and as we approached the Kapi I could feel the energy change and it began to swirl around us.

It was very interesting to feel the different energies between both areas. The ancestral guardians were certainly present, protecting these two majestic locations at the base of the Rock.

* * *

On the day that we visited Uluru, the weather was perfect. The sun was shining and there were a few puffy clouds floating in the sky above us. I have to say that, as this was the first time I had ever been to Uluru, I wondered why I had taken so long to pay this incredible location a visit. I fell totally in love with Uluru and its gorgeous energy.

We walked back to the pick-up area and made it back just in time for our return bus trip. I felt so uplifted by my first visit to Uluru, I couldn't wait for the up-coming tours and adventures we had planned over the next week.

* * *

The following day we were picked up at 4.30 a.m. for a bus tour to Kings Canyon. The morning was quite cold as we boarded the bus. The drive to Kings Canyon was approximately 3 1/2, which gave us a chance to catch up on some sleep.

We arrived at Kings Creek Station where we had a hearty home-cooked Aussie breakfast. Once breakfast was finished, we boarded the bus to reach our destination. There were two types of walks that we could do on the day of the tour. The choices were Kings Creek or the Kings Canyon Rim walk.

We chose to walk the Kings Canyon Rim. This walk is a 6 km moderate-to-difficult loop that takes 3–4 hours. The most intimidating part of the walk is the steep stairs that lead up to the top of the canyon. There are over 500 stairs to climb, but the view at the top is very spectacular. I am terrified of heights so, for me, looking up was the only way forward.

I did see some feathers on the way up the stairs, and they gave me encouragement that I was going to be fine; I knew that my angels were not far from my side. Once we reached the top of the canyon we began our beautiful walk along the Canyon Rim. The scenery at the top of the rim is diverse: there are trees and palms growing in areas you wouldn't think it was possible for a plant to grow. In some areas the landscape looks like something on Mars – quite arid and with rocks and boulders strewn throughout. The drop from the top of the rim of the canyon to the ground below is around 15 m; more in different locations. We arrived at a location named 'Kestrel Falls'.

Our tour guide warned everyone not to go too close to the edge. He said that a backpacker had died at this location while trying to take a photograph. The backpacker had been posing for a prank photograph when they overstepped the edge and fell to their death. I felt an overwhelming sadness and despair here. I couldn't believe how my feelings of happiness had suddenly disappeared. For the rest of the walk I felt that I wasn't alone. I began to feel the energy of a young blonde woman who had an English accent. The young woman felt a similar age to my children and I could feel that she was very excited that I was able to sense, see and feel her presence. At the time our guide spoke of the accidental death, he didn't mention anything about whether or not the person who died was male or female; he hadn't described their age or their nationality. Once we returned to the resort I could still hear, see and feel a young female energy around me.

We decided to go for dinner at Gecko's Café. While we were waiting for our food to arrive I began to tell my husband about the young woman I felt around me. I told him that I felt that the young woman was a similar age to our children and I could see that she had blonde hair, blue eyes and a big, beautiful smile. I told him that I felt she was sad because of how she had died so tragically and how she worried about her family.

While we waited for our meal to arrive I decided to look up the incident on my iPhone. The image of the young woman appeared. It was the same young woman I had been seeing since our visit to Kings Canyon.

I could instantly feel the sadness of the young lady and that of her loving parents. The beautiful young lady was 23 at the time of her death. Her death was not only tragic but also a very unnecessary waste of life. She had tried to jump down to a ledge when she had lost her balance and then she stumbled as she tried to reach for the ledge. She had then rolled onto a rocky protrusion before falling a distance of 15 m onto more rocks below. She suffered life-threatening injuries of skull fractures, bleeding to the brain, a broken back, fractured pelvis and a fractured right shoulder blade.

Unfortunately, it had taken rangers over 50 minutes to arrive at the scene of the accident and she died soon after their arrival. What seemed so tragic was that the endeavour to photograph an image that seemed to be on the edge was why a beautiful young lady died.

As I showed my husband the image of her, we spoke to each other about the tragic event. As parents ourselves we couldn't even begin to contemplate the loss to her parents. We both spoke about how life is so fragile and you just never know when it is your time. You could be in the prime of your life, living the life you feel you are meant to live, when it can be just so swiftly taken without a second glance.

Little did we know how we would both be challenging our own longevity within the next 24 hours.

* * *

That night it was time to do the astro-photography course as part of the Astronomy weekend. I went along by myself as Warwick was not at all interested in standing in the dark with a camera.

Well, what a disaster. I did everything that I was told by our astronomer and I had previously watched the YouTube videos for the camera settings. I thought that I had everything right. When I took the photographs they looked okay in the viewfinder. However, when I looked at the photographs upon getting back to the hotel room, I was greatly disappointed. Every photograph I had taken was blurry. I truly began to question if I was meant to be at Uluru for what was planned to be a very special week of photography. I had planned for this weekend, and everything that could not work was now not working. I can see you reading this saying that if you are so psychic why didn't you know that this would happen. Yes, I am a positive person and I always look at the good in everything. Yes, everything is for a reason, so I was prepared that things could only get better. Or, could they?

Luckily, (or unluckily) one of the highlights of our trip was to take place the following day. We had booked to go on the Field of Lights Helicopter Experience. I have been in a helicopter three times before. Yes, I am terrified of heights and yet nothing was going to let this fear stop me from going in that helicopter.

In the morning, Warwick and I decided to go for a walk around the resort. As you know by now, my beautiful father-in-law comes to visit us, as a magpie. As we were walking along a bush track we both saw a single magpie sitting in a tree close to the track. It was happily singing away in the tree. Let me remind you that in Uluru there are not many birds around, least of all magpies. I said to Warwick that it was a sign that his beautiful dad was with us and that he wanted us to know that he was looking after us.

Thank goodness that magpie showed up that day as I truly feel that it was due to my father-in-law and our guardian angels that we are both alive today.

In the afternoon we were making our way to the front of the resort to be picked up by the helicopter for the 'Field of Lights' Dinner Adventure. I felt really nervous and I was quite concerned about the helicopter. I expressed this to Warwick and he told me that I was just worrying too much and everything would be okay. When we arrived at the front our pilot was already waiting for us. Unfortunately, the hotel had written

*'Pop' gave me a sign from above during my trip. This is a lone magpie
that we saw at Uluru before we went on our helicopter encounter*

down the wrong time for the pick-up on our itinerary and the pilot
informed us that we were fifteen minutes late. By now the feeling of
unsettledness started to become more of an issue for me. I truly hate to
be running late, especially when it isn't my fault. I was really beginning
to question whether or not this planned helicopter flight over Kata Tjuta
and Uluru was a good idea.

We arrived at the helicopter base were given our helicopter safety briefing. My nervousness was now beginning to make me feel really uncomfortable, but I chose to ignore the feeling as it was time to board our flight.

Our pilot ran through his safety checks and then he attempted to start the helicopter. It took three attempts for the helicopter to start. It initially sounded like the helicopter had a flat battery. A little voice in my head was telling me at this stage that we shouldn't fly. I began to have an overwhelming feeling of sheer and utter dread.

The pilot pushed the ignition button one more time and then the helicopter jumped to life. I felt that the best way to overcome my anxiety was to call in my angels and ask for their protection during the flight. I was wearing a tiny little necklace with angel wings on it, my trusted 'prayer for the angel's' bracelet was on my wrist, and my beautiful angel medallion I bought in England was hanging around my neck. I had angels all over me. I kept trying to think happy thoughts and hoped that everything would be okay. I tried to focus on this being a once-in-a-lifetime adventure.

The helicopter rose in the air and we headed towards Kata Tjuta. The feeling of this helicopter was very different to what I had experienced before. The flight was not as smooth; the helicopter kind of vibrated and the energy felt a little strange. I forced my attention on the surrounding view and began to take photographs of the beautiful scenery below.

I was using my Canon EOS 7D to take the photographs and my back-up was my iPhone 6s. I began snapping as many images as I could because I knew that this was a special moment. After all, this was part of my bucket list. We had just arrived in the area of Kata Tjuta when my camera jammed up. I remember feeling quite annoyed that I was just in the right spot for the perfect picture and then the camera wouldn't work. I turned the camera on and off, to no avail. I quickly started to take

This is a photograph of us approaching Kata Jutu before our helicopter began to sound the warning alarm. At this time both my Canon camera and iPhone froze

photographs with my phone. Suddenly the same thing happened to the camera on the phone: it jammed and the screen went completely white.

I looked towards the dashboard of the helicopter and an orange light began to flash and there was a beeping noise. The voice in my head said: 'I told you something wasn't right!' Our pilot first told us that we might have a faulty switch and that he would monitor the situation. He did a check of the equipment and then he said that we might need to cut our flight short and return to base if the warning alarm continued to sound. I immediately said to him that I knew that something was wrong, which I am sure was something he did not want to hear. He responded that there was an issue with the governor on the helicopter and it was affecting the RPM. I instantly replied to him that I had had a gut feeling the entire day that something was going to happen to us while we were in the helicopter. Our pilot then said that there was no need for alarm – he had everything under control. He then turned the helicopter around and we began to head back to base. I continued to take photographs. By this stage both the phone and camera were now working again. I also kept summoning in my angels as I truly was worried about how we were going to land.

The warning light and beeper began to sound again and then our pilot said that he had to struggle to keep up the RPM. The helicopter began to vibrate more than it had previously and I began to get really anxious.

This is where we made our emergency landing. Back safe on the ground. Saved by an Angel

The pilot made the decision to try for an emergency landing. As the vegetation near Kata Tjuta is quite rocky in places, our pilot decided to head the helicopter towards a dirt road that we could see in the distance. The pilot radioed to base to tell them about our impending emergency; he gave the details about where we were heading. The warning light and beeper were now sounding every few seconds and I was really getting concerned. I thought that I might as well keep taking photographs – if this was to be the end there would be images on my phone that might tell the story of what had happened. Pity I wasn't thinking enough to record the whole event on the video on my phone.

The pilot started to descend towards the road and my heart was well and truly in my mouth. All I can remember seeing is the land appearing quickly beneath us. I didn't know whether or not to be excited that we were going to land, or to brace myself for a crash back to earth.

All I remember is that I was calling on every single angel I could muster. I have had near-death experiences in the past, through medical events, but nothing like this. I began to think of how many helicopter emergency landings that end badly are reported on the news. I hoped that the three of us were not going to make the headlines for the same reason.

Suddenly, the ground was just beneath us, and the helicopter landed on the ground safely. I can't begin to tell you how pleased I was. I just wanted to get out and lie down on the ground and kiss the earth. The adrenalin that was surging through me felt incredible. My husband and I gave each other a big hug as it truly dawned on us just how lucky we were.

Our pilot was wonderful and we couldn't thank him enough for getting us safely back on the ground, in one piece. The pilot radioed back to base to tell them what had happened. The operator at the other end had said that someone had reported seeing the helicopter landing in an unusual area and the emergency services had been alerted. It was good to know that we were in safe hands and that someone was aware of our situation. It also reminded us of what could have been.

Our pilot asked for someone to pick us up from our current location and transport us back to civilisation. We were asked whether or not we wanted to continue our planned night at the 'Field of Lights' or whether we wanted to return to our hotel. We chose to visit the 'Field of Lights' exhibition at the foot of Uluru. The manager of the helicopter company came and picked the three of us up and we were then dropped at the exhibition. We were told that someone would be meeting us at the location, as there were large groups on buses, arriving at the same time. We were met and sent up to an observation area to have drinks and watch the sunset.

Little did we know that we had been sent to the wrong location. About ten minutes later a man came looking for us and led us into the right area. We were led off to the 'Field of Lights' and then asked why we were late. We explained our situation and a number of people wanted to talk to us about what we had just experienced. Two men who were retired helicopter pilots came over to us. They were so excited and they asked us what type of landing we had experienced. To be honest I didn't know the answer to that question. All I was really focussing on was reaching the ground in one piece. The men explained how lucky we were to have landed without any issues and to be alive to tell our story. All I could do was thank my angels for assisting in keeping us safe and alive to tell the tale.

The organisers of the 'Field of Lights' dinner then came to put everyone into dining groups and we were led to our tables. As we were walking to our delegated table I saw a beautiful white feather on the red earth beneath me. I remember thinking that I was yet again receiving a sign that my angels were telling me that everything was okay.

I truly felt extremely blessed that my angels are with me no matter when or where I need them. I know that the only thing that truly matters is that I believe and that they will find a way to show me they are there.

During dinner I really realised the enormity of what we had just gone through. We both spoke about how blessed we were to be the parents of three amazing children. We felt even more blessed that we were allowed to stay on Earth longer, to still be part of their lives.

The gift we had both been given brought tears to my eyes and I began to contemplate what the outcome could have been. I am normally a very positive person, but this experience did shake my positivity just a little bit. However, as I am still here to write about it, I am sure that you will understand how thankful I truly am to be able to finish the tale.

* * *

After the dinner we walked through the 'Field of Lights' exhibition. I wasn't really in the best state to appreciate the magic that was before me. I do have plans to go back to Uluru and this time I hope to photograph the 'Field of Lights' in its entirety.

After our helicopter experience we still had two days left in Uluru. The following day we had a sunrise tour. We had to get up really early, but it was so worth it. We visited Uluru at sunrise and we were privileged to then visit Kata Tjuta on foot. I felt so happy to be alive to be able to experience what spiritual places Kata Tjuta and Uluru truly are.

On our return to the resort we thought that we would pay the helicopter company a visit, to discuss the previous day. The people at the office had heard about our experience and they told us that the company would be in touch. The staff assured us that we were very lucky to be alive to tell the story. They said that what we had experienced was really rare. This didn't make us feel any better. All my husband and I could think was how lucky we were to be alive.

* * *

The helicopter company didn't bother to contact us while we were at Uluru. It wasn't until I wrote a Tripadvisor review about our experience that I was contacted — a week after our return to Sydney. The only reason I was contacted by the company was to be asked to remove my review. The manager was more concerned about his reputation than he was about our safety and welfare.

* * *

When we got back to the resort, the weather began to take a turn for the worse and storm clouds gathered into a huge storm. We decided, as it was our last day, that we would try and hire a car to visit the Rock one last time. We were lucky to be able to rent the last rental car that was available.

As we drove towards Uluru the rain poured down. Even though the weather was dreadful, we marvelled at what a gift from above we were both being given. Uluru doesn't experience rain all that much throughout the year, so you can imagine how special this was.

Even though I wasn't able to capture images during our 'Field of Lights' visit, we were able to capture the most amazing images of waterfalls on Uluru and then Kata Tjuta. I truly felt that the angels from above did protect us and they also put on a natural show of spirit, through the images we captured on the 'Rock'.

* * *

Through all of my experiences I can't thank my angels enough. I truly believe in angels and I am happy that they also believe in me (otherwise I might not be here today).

To all of you who question your angels, my only word to you is: 'Believe'.

CHAPTER 10

Butterfly Kisses

Teresa Cummings was born in 1926 at St. Margaret's Hospital in Sydney. Teresa was my maternal grandmother, who led a rather adventurous life. During my Nanna's life she changed her name to Mary Theresa. Sadly, at the age of 78, she passed away. This is her story.

Mary's life-long best friend was Nell. The pair met in their late teens and they remained friends until Mary's passing. Nell was the sister of Mary's first husband, William 'Bill' Duncan. Duncan was the surname she carried with her throughout her life. In our family we called our grandmothers 'Nanna' and then their surnames. So from this point forward I will call her Nanna, or Nanna Duncan.

Nell had a big influence on Nanna's life. She was always extremely close to my mum and her brother, Brien. Nell was like an aunt to our family. As a child, I would go with Nanna to visit 'Auntie Nell' at her home in the eastern suburbs. Nell and her husband, Bob, retired to the

Left to right: Mary Theresa Duncan and Nell Austic (née Duncan)

Gold Coast when I was in my teens. Once she moved I didn't get to see her very often.

Nanna Duncan was always full of life; she was a free spirit and was always on the move. As a child I remember going to visit her and asking my mother why she was now living at a different house. My mother would just smile and tell me that she had moved again. As I got older I realised that this was just who she was. I like to think of Nanna as a 'Rolling stone that gathered no moss!'

Nanna was one of nine children and she had a very challenging life. She became a single mother at the age of seventeen when she gave birth to my beautiful mother, Leonie. Nanna married William 'Bill' Duncan, and a year later she gave birth to William Brien Duncan. After the marriage, Bill Duncan adopted my mother, Leonie.

Unfortunately for Nanna and the children, the marriage didn't last. Nanna was never lucky in love and she experienced heartache many times in her life. During her life, one of her partners attacked her, beating her to within an inch of her life. She suffered a fractured skull and a broken jaw, as well as other facial injuries. Nanna was in hospital in a coma for two weeks before regaining consciousness. Thankfully she survived this brutal attack, however it wasn't until she was older that the damage she sustained in the attack would come back to hinder her health and subsequently attribute to her death.

When I was nine years old, Nanna was living in Glebe in Sydney's inner west. One night she was crossing the road when she was involved in a serious car accident. The weather on this evening was quite miserable; it was raining heavily and Nanna crossed the road in front of a taxi. Due to the poor visibility on that night the taxi driver didn't see her and she was hit. She had both her kneecaps and her shoulder broken, as well as suffering numerous cuts and abrasions. When my family heard of the dreadful news I wondered if I would ever see my Nanna again. Thankfully, after many weeks in hospital, lots of physiotherapy and rehabilitation, Nanna was allowed to go home. No matter what challenges were thrown at Nanna she always bounced back with a smile on her face. She was so full of life that I thought she was going to live forever.

When Nanna retired, she moved to the Gold Coast in Queensland with her long-term partner, Sean, to be near Auntie Nell. Nanna always loved the beach, so this was a perfect opportunity for her to be close to Nell and to be near the coast.

Sean was a very controlling man and he was very jealous of our family connection to Nanna. Sean liked there to be distance between Nanna and my family as it gave him a greater control over her. Over the years we began to see Nanna less and less. This was exactly what Sean wanted, although we did have weekly contact with Nanna via the phone. Whenever she called she always tried to sound happy, even though there was an underlying sadness in her voice.

One year I organised a holiday to the Gold Coast, with Warwick and the children. I booked accommodation only a few streets away from Nanna so that we could be close to her. We were so excited to be able to spend time with her. My childhood memories of her were of a fun-loving lady, who loved her children and grandchildren.

When we arrived at the Gold Coast we promptly went to her house to visit, only to be told that we weren't welcome in her home because Sean didn't want us to bother her. The trip had been planned for many months; Sean and Nanna had been aware that we were coming to visit, so Sean's greeting was quite a shock.

I will never forget the disappointed looks on the children's faces when Sean told us all to go away. We had just driven over 700 km from Sydney to the Gold Coast for a special trip to see Nanna. Prior to leaving for our trip the children had drawn pictures and made a friendship bracelet to give Nanna as a special surprise.

Sean only allowed Nanna to come to the door to give the kids a hug and to accept the children's presents, then he made her go back inside. During the next two weeks of our holiday we were only allowed to see Nanna once more. Sean was in control.

The next time we saw Nanna was at Christmas a few years later, at my parents' home. During this time it was evident that Nanna's health was on the decline. Nanna had symptoms of a frozen shoulder, which then worsened to symptoms similar to that of Motor Neuron disease. After further medical investigation, the doctors discovered that she had a form of palsy that was brought on by the attack and car accident that she had experienced years earlier.

The last time I saw Nanna alive was when I flew up to Queensland to film an episode of *Sensing Murder*. Rhonda Byrne, the head of Prime Time Productions, graciously allowed me to fly into the Gold Coast a day ahead of our filming schedule so I could visit my beautiful Nanna.

On this particular occasion Sean allowed me to spend a few hours with her. This precious time we had together I will never forget.

Nanna's favourite chocolates were Darrell Lea chocolate-coated ginger pieces. I bought a bag of them for her, as a special surprise. Even though Nanna had great trouble swallowing them, due to the palsy, she had a wonderful time trying to eat the chocolates. It was quite hard to communicate with her, however I understood that, by hook or by crook, she was going to eat the chocolate ginger, even if I had to cut it into tiny pieces for her.

Even though her illness had ravaged her body I could still see light within her eyes. When I was a child Nanna would always joke with me that when she died she would come back and haunt us. My Nanna was always loudly spoken and she said that if she did make it to Heaven we would always be able to hear her from the other side. One of the last things she said to me was: 'Don't worry, "Bibbie G" (my nickname). I will come back and haunt you.'

When Nanna's health went into a quick decline, Sean gained greater control of her, causing her to be more isolated from the family. Nanna's healthy mind became trapped in a body that would no longer respond to her commands. Little by little, her speech, mobility and any control of her limbs, were taken away. The one thing in life my Nanna loved was eating. When it got to the point that she couldn't even perform the simple task of feeding herself, she gave up her will to live.

My mum, Leonie, went up to stay with Nanna in Queensland to nurse her before she passed, but Sean made it so difficult for Mum to be there that she had to abandon her attempt to spend her final time with her. A few weeks after Mum returned home, Nanna was put into hospital, where she died from a heart attack and other complications. Her loss was devastating to the family, but most of all to my mum.

On the day of Nanna's funeral I flew up to the Gold Coast. This was a very challenging time as both my boys are born a day apart and Sean had decided to have Nanna's funeral on Ryan's birthday! Therefore, I was only able to be in Queensland for the day. The whole funeral was a surreal experience. As I was standing in front of everybody, giving the eulogy, I could see Nanna sitting in the front row smiling at me, looking very much alive and well. I noticed her looking behind, to check out who had shown up. The most amusing thing to see was when Sean got up to speak about her life. He said that a certain song was her favourite song. I watched as she yelled at him: 'No, it's not. I always hated that song. It's your favourite, not mine!' I started laughing to myself, but tried not to make it obvious as I knew that nobody else could hear what she was saying. At least Nanna hadn't lost any of her cheeky personality since transitioning into the spirit world.

Nanna wanted me to pass on messages to my family, especially my mum. The most important thing she wanted to pass on to everyone was that she wasn't suffering anymore. Nanna looked better than I had seen her for many years, once she transitioned into spirit. She was able-bodied, able to speak, and as cheeky as she always had been. She winked at me and said to me: 'You knew that you would hear me from the other side!' I certainly could hear her – loud and clear.

When the funeral finished, everyone left for a wake at Nanna's local club. It was lovely to see that Nanna came, too. I was so happy to catch up with Auntie Nell.

Nanna was concerned for all of her family and friends. I watched as she sat with loved ones when they spoke of the cherished memories they had shared with her. Nanna seemed so proud that so many people loved her. She told me that next time round she would do things differently. She would prefer to have the wake first and die later, leaving this life with one great party.

After Nanna passed I tried to keep in touch with her partner, Sean, even though he was a very cold and challenging man. I thought that no matter how difficult Sean was, out of respect I would try to keep in touch with him, for Nanna. However, the family went through many challenges with Sean after her passing.

Nanna's wishes were for her to be cremated instead of being buried. Sean chose to keep her ashes with him at their unit, even though my mother and uncle wanted their mother to be interred at a cemetery, with a plaque as a memorial to her.

My mum suffered terribly with her loss and she was haunted by a feeling that she wished she had done more for Nanna. Sean had his own ideas about how Nanna would be remembered, however. The one thing that saddened me most was that after Nanna's funeral I hardly ever heard or felt her presence. I thought, of all of the people who I had lost, Nanna would be the easiest one to make contact with. She promised that she would always be with me and that I would always be able to hear her; but this was not to be.

Sean was eventually moved into a nursing home. When he moved from their apartment, Nanna's ashes had mysteriously vanished, never to be found. This was the final blow for my mum. Mum was devastated that, yet again, Sean was still in control of Nanna and her final wishes.

* * *

Almost ten years later I was working in my garden and Nanna's face kept popping into my head. I always find when I am amongst nature that those in spirit find time to make contact with me. It was a pleasant surprise to have Nanna visit. Since Nanna's passing I really hadn't had much contact with her, except for at the funeral and her wake. On this particular day

Nanna was showing me how sad Mum was and she wanted me to let Mum know that she was okay in spirit.

Nanna wanted me to tell Mum not to worry about her ashes because they were only a remnant of the person she was. She said it was more important for me to let Mum know that Nanna's soul had survived and that she was now alive and well, in spirit. As Nanna was speaking with me a beautiful black-and-blue butterfly flew around me. I asked Nanna if this was a sign from her and she said that from this day forward, whenever any of the family saw a butterfly, to see it as a sign that Nanna had come to visit.

Butterflies are a very significant symbol of the transition of life into the spirit world. A butterfly is such a beautiful, ethereal creature that flits from one flower to the next. A butterfly signifies freedom and movement and to me this was a perfect representation of Nanna's life because she was always such a free spirit.

I was so thankful that Nanna had finally found a way to come back to me, from spirit. It was at this moment the idea of organising a butterfly release for my Nanna's memorial came to mind. I decided, as a surprise to Mum, that I would organise a special memorial in celebration of Nanna's life, to be held on the 10th anniversary of her passing.

Over the next few weeks I researched how I could find somewhere to buy some butterflies (if that was at all possible). The internet is such a wonderful place to find anything you want – even butterflies. I discovered a lovely gentleman who runs a business called Butterfly Encounters, situated in Indooroopilly, Queensland. He breeds butterflies for all types of occasions. I made a phone call to him and explained the memorial I was arranging for my Nanna. He assured me that arranging the butterflies wasn't going to be a problem because he breeds the butterflies specifically for each occasion. He explained that it would take six weeks to breed the butterflies, from eggs to winged beauties.

My only remaining question was how I was going to get the butterflies from Queensland to the Central Coast of NSW, for the butterfly release. He assured me that this was the least of my worries, so I ordered twelve butterflies for the release, one butterfly for each family member attending the memorial, and one for Nanna. From the moment I began to organise the memorial I saw butterflies everywhere. I felt that this was confirmation from Nanna that I was doing what she wanted.

The Monarch butterfly I released for Nanna

I rang Mum to tell her about my idea and she became very excited. Mum and Dad arranged a memorial plaque in memory of Nanna, for the cemetery. In a quiet leafy corner of the cemetery there is a beautiful memorial wall covered in brass vine leaves with the names of loved ones in spirit. Mum and Dad chose to purchase a leaf on this wall. They were also given permission to release the butterflies at the cemetery, so now everything was in place for Nanna's memorial.

The butterflies were sent from Queensland via Express Post. Each butterfly was packed in its own individual release envelope, accompanied with cotton-wool packing and ice packs. Our biggest concern was whether the butterflies would survive the trip from Queensland to the Central Coast. Thankfully, our precious cargo arrived, ready for the release, the day before the memorial. My family met at the cemetery. My brother, Michael, sister-in-law Jocelyn and my beautiful niece Ashley and nephew Rhys joined my parents, my husband and children for the release.

It was a day that I am sure none of us will ever forget. I explained to everyone that this was the day that we could finally give Nanna the send-off she so rightly deserved. As a family we would now have a place to remember Nanna, which we could visit since her ashes had mysteriously disappeared. The day was extremely hot and humid. I prayed that all of the butterflies would still be alive in their release envelopes when it was time to open them and set them free. The butterflies we released were Monarch butterflies. They were orange and black and, with their open wing span, were approximately the size of a tea cup.

Within the grounds of the cemetery there is a beautiful man-made waterfall. Adjacent to that area is a garden and lawn area that is full of flowering plants and shrubs. We chose to release the butterflies in this area because we felt it would give them the best chance of survival.

Well, I am happy to report that as each of us carefully opened our precious envelopes all twelve butterflies were alive and well. On opening the envelopes each butterfly proudly stood up on its release envelope, stretched its legs and wings and then took flight. Some of the butterflies stayed and flew around us for about an hour. I will never forget the joy on everyone's faces when each individual's butterfly took flight.

The Monarch butterfly I released for Nanna

We all rejoiced in our memories of Nanna and knew that she would be standing with us when her spirit was set free. The other wonderful thing about having the butterfly release is that we used butterflies that were native to the local area, so the release was going to give the butterflies a chance to breed and carry on their lifecycle.

After the release we all visited the vine-leaf memorial wall, where Nanna's leaf was now positioned. We sent our prayers and thoughts to Nanna and hoped she knew just how much she truly meant to us all. I also hoped that this event would now help my mum with the overwhelming grief she had suffered for the past ten years. I gave Mum a butterfly pendant in memory of Nanna, to remind her of this special day.

* * *

In late 2016, Auntie Nell had begun to suffer some health issues and moved back to Sydney to be close to her family. Her husband, Bob, had passed away some years before and she was living alone in her home on the Gold Coast. Nell moved into a retirement home that had once been St. Margaret's Hospital, where Nanna had been born. It was wonderful to reconnect with Auntie Nell. The last time I had seen her was at Nanna's funeral. Both Nanna and Nell were very similar in nature. Seeing Auntie Nell reminded me of my childhood and the times I went with Nanna to visit her.

Whenever I visited Auntie Nell, I loved how she would recount stories about her and Nanna when they were young ladies. Some of the stories she told me gave me a new insight to my gorgeous Nanna and the life she lived. Auntie Nell was one of my biggest fans; she told me how much she loved my books and most of all she loved my angel cards. She told me that she used them every day to get a positive message from her angels. I felt so proud that she was open to the type of work that I do. Seeing Auntie Nell made me feel close, both to her and Nanna, once again. Each time I visited Auntie Nell, Nanna would appear in the room with us and I could give Auntie Nell messages from her. At times when I was speaking with Auntie Nell, her beloved husband, Bob, would suddenly appear behind her. Uncle Bob would ask me to relay messages to her, letting her know that he was always by her side and how much he loved and missed her.

Auntie Nell told me how happy she was that I could communicate with them both. Each time I visited her she said to me that she knew that she would be with them both again in the not-too-distant future. At the time I told her that I didn't want to hear her say that. I wanted to spend more time with her before she left this Earth.

I told Auntie Nell about the butterfly release that I had organised for Nanna on the 10th anniversary of her passing. Auntie Nell cheekily said to me that when she passed she would come back with Nanna as a butterfly, too. She said that I'd need to look out for two butterflies instead of just one.

* * *

The last time I saw Auntie Nell, Mum and I had met her for lunch. We took her out to a café around the corner from where she lived. Even though Auntie Nell had a walker, nothing held her back from achieving anything that she wanted to do. We had a wonderful lunch and I have this memory to treasure forever.

After we returned to Auntie Nell's room, we bid her farewell and I told her I would come back and see her the next week. Unfortunately I became sick with the flu and didn't want to visit while I was sick. I then made plans to visit her a few weeks later. I didn't get to meet up with her again. She passed away in her sleep in August 2017.

I was devastated to hear the news of her passing, even though I knew that she had been waiting to reconnect with her loved ones in spirit. I feel blessed to have reconnected with her; Auntie Nell was a tiny little lady who had a big heart and a huge personality.

While Auntie Nell was alive I had told her how sad I had been that I couldn't connect with Nanna after her funeral. It was only through meeting up with Auntie Nell again that Nanna made contact with me. I am sure that Auntie Nell paid close attention to what I had said. From the moment she passed I could hear her loud and clear. She told me how happy she was to be with Nanna and Bob. In the days leading up to her funeral she was in constant contact with me. The precious memories we shared together are something I will always cherish. I also thank her for helping me to hear Nanna once again.

On the day of her funeral Auntie Nell told me that I wasn't allowed to wear all black because that was far too morbid. She told me that I had to wear a pink top. I did as she told me and wore a black jacket, pink floral top and black pants. Thankfully she approved of this. When I arrived at the funeral, the hearse arrived with a baby pink coffin inside. I couldn't help but smile. Pink was her favourite colour and I always knew that she would want to leave this world in style.

During the service I could see her with her beloved Bob and my Nanna by her side. I am sure Bob and Nanna wanted me to reconnect with Auntie Nell so that she knew that they would meet her when it was time for her to go.

* * *

It is now six years since our butterfly memorial release. Whenever any of the family makes contact with Nanna and Nell, we can't wait to tell each other of the adventures we have had with butterflies. I am sure that Nanna is quite busy in spirit, orchestrating to have butterflies visit all family members. All of us look at butterflies in a new light. Many people would view butterflies as pretty insects that flit around in the garden. But when butterflies come and pay a visit, I know that it is Nanna and Auntie Nell visiting from above, sharing butterfly kisses from beyond. I know that they are together again, being as cheeky as ever.

In Memory of Mary Theresa Davidson

'Nanna Dunk' and 'Bub'

You have given me wings with which to fly

Now I breathe in deep and spread them wide

into the wind where the butterflies glide.

Don't weep today, for I am not there,

I've a date with a butterfly to dance in the air.

I'll be singing in the sunshine, wild and free,

playing tag with the wind, while I'm waiting for thee.

We are as the wings of a butterfly,

bound together with our love soaring on high.

Acknowledgements

It is always wonderful to be able to share the stories of those in spirit, with the living. *Always With You – Messages From Beyond* has been a labour of love that I have the privilege of sharing with you.

I would firstly like to thank John Boardman, Peter Bussler, Jessica and Anne Sommerville, Tas Psarakis, Sophia and Victor Shaw, whose touching stories have made this book possible. It has been such an enlightening experience to meet and communicate with you and your loved ones in spirit.

Each of your touching stories has been a pleasure to write, the lengths that your loved ones have gone to, to make contact, are very touching and extremely personal.

To Debbie Brown, thank you for your guidance with this manuscript. I loved having you as part of my team. You are an angel.

To my gorgeous family: Warwick, Ryan, Blake and Shannon. Thank you for having the patience to let me see this book through to the end. I know it seems like I am always on the computer writing and in another world. Without your support I would not be able to do what I do. I love you all so much.

To Lisa and Paul at Rockpool Publishing, it is yet again a pleasure to work with you on this book. I look forward to working with you in the future with new ideas and projects. Thank you for believing in me.

Last, but not least, to my manager, Richard Martin, thank you for your patience and understanding while I undertake the writing process. Your encouragement always gets me through, even when I have 'writers block'. Together we make a great team.

To the public, thank you for your support and encouragement over the years. I hope that you will enjoy *Always With You* as much as I have enjoyed writing it.

About the Author

Sydney-based Debbie Malone, the 2013 Australian Psychic of the Year, is an acclaimed and highly respected psychic, clairvoyant, psychometry expert and spirit medium.

Debbie assists police Australia-wide to solve murder investigations and missing persons' cases. She conducts private readings and workshops on how to tune into the spirit world, and is regularly interviewed in national print and on television and radio. Television appearances include *Today Tonight, Sensing Murder, Sunrise, Today, The Project* and most recently *The One.*

Her extraordinary gift has enabled her to receive visions from both the living and the dead, from the past, present and future, and to convey messages to bereaved families from their departed loved ones. Debbie also specialises in paranormal spirit photography.

Debbie's book *Awaken Your Psychic Ability* was published in 2016, followed by *Clues from Beyond: Insights from the living and from the dead* and *Never Alone* in 2017.

Debbie has also created a series of bestselling Angel cards – *Angel Whispers, Angel Wishes, Angels to Watch Over You, Angel Reading Cards* and *Guardian Angel Reading Cards.*

Debbie Malone's gift has enabled her to see beyond the here and now and she draws strength from using the world of spirit to help herself and others, and from knowing that we are never alone.

www.betweentwoworlds.net

Other books by Debbie ...

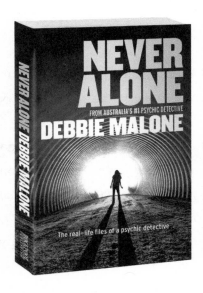

Never Alone:
The real—life files of a
psychic detective

ISBN: 978-1-925429-54-1

This book takes readers on the roller—coaster ride of Debbie's journey, from receiving confirmation of her capacities after a miscarriage at the age of twenty—eight, to volunteering her services to the police on high—profile cases.

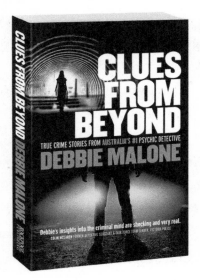

Clues From Beyond:
Insights from the living
and from the dead

ISBN: 978-1-925429-47-3

In *Clues From Beyond*, Debbie shares more personal experiences with the spirit world, conveys messages from the departed and describes the ripple effect they create in extending proof that life and love still go on across the veil.

Available at all good bookstores or online at
www.rockpoolpublishing.com.au